ADDING VALUE?

ADDING VALUE?
School's responsibility for pupils' personal development

Edited by
Sally Inman and Martin Buck

Trentham Books
for the Centre for Cross Curricular Initiatives

First published in 1995 by Trentham Books Limited

Trentham Books Limited
Westview House
734 London Road
Oakhill
Stoke-on-Trent
Staffordshire
England ST4 5NP

British Cataloguing in Publication Data
A catalogue record for this book is available from the British Library
ISBN: 1 85856 044 6

Cover design by Shawn Stipling

Designed and typeset by Trentham Print Design Ltd., Chester and printed in Great Britain by BPC Wheatons Ltd, Exeter

Contents

Acknowledgements   vii

Notes on Contributors   ix

Introduction
Martin Buck and Sally Inman   xi

Chapter 1
Setting a framework for personal development
Martin Buck and Sally Inman   1

Chapter 2
Equal opportunities and personal development
Helena Burke   31

Chapter 3
Race and cultural diversity
Pauline Lyseight-jones   47

Chapter 4
Towards some understandings of sexuality education
Brenda Hanson and Paul Patrick   67

Chapter 5
**Citizenship education — more than a forgotten
cross-curricular theme?**
Martin Buck and Sally Inman   85

Chapter 6
Reading, Identity and Personal Development
Elizabeth Plackett   115

Chapter 7
Making sense of the spiritual and moral
Lynne Broadbent 131

Chapter 8
Futures Education: Citizenship for Today and Tommorrow
David Hicks 143

Chapter 9
The future basis for a 14-19 entitlement?
Michael Young 161

Postscript 181

Acknowledgements

The editors would like to thank all those teachers and LEA Advisers who have been involved with the Centre for Cross Curricular Initiatives, Goldsmiths College, University of London. Their contributions have greatly helped to develop our work. Thanks to the Management Committee of the Centre for their continued support. We are grateful to those HMIs who have developed ideas around the spiritual, moral, social and cultural development of pupils. This work has greatly benefited our own thinking.

A special thanks to Judith Bretherton, whose able administration has enabled this work to be sustained and to Gillian Klein for giving the final manuscript a sharper focus.

Notes on contributors

Lynne Broadbent is Senior Lecturer in Religious Education at Canterbury Christ Church College. She formerly lectured at Goldsmiths College, University of London, and at the West London Institute of Higher Education. She has considerable experience of working with teachers and students in the primary and secondary sectors in the areas of Religious, Personal, Social and Moral Education. She has written and edited resources materials for use in primary and secondary classrooms.

Helena Burke has taught in inner city schools for eight years, where she has been actively involved in issues of equal opportunity. She is currently a lecturer in education at Goldsmiths College, where she convenes the PGCE Secondary Social Studies/Humanities course.

Martin Buck is Headteacher of Gayton High School in Harrow. He was previously Inspector with Ealing Education Department and has been a Deputy Headteacher in an inner London school. He is co-author (with Sally Inman) of *Curriculum Guidance No 1: Whole School Provision for Personal and Social Development* 1992 and *Curriculum Guidance No 2: Re-affirming Values* 1993, both published by the Centre for Cross Curricular Initiatives, Goldsmiths College.

Brenda Hanson has taught in London schools since 1979. She has taught science and PSHE and is currently in charge of Key Stage 3 science in a south-east London Comprehensive. She is a founder member of the Black Teachers Group at her present school. She has previously been in charge of health education and has led many initiatives on anti-racist delivery of health education.

David Hicks is Lecturer and Research Fellow in the Faculty of Education at Bath College of Higher Education. He is an international authority on the need for a global perspective and futures dimension in the curriculum and has worked extensively in the UK, Italy, Australia and Canada. His most recent book, with Cathie Holden, is *Visions of the Future: Why We Need to Teach for Tomorrow* (Trentham, 1995).

Sally Inman is Senior Lecturer and Head of Professional Development within the Department of Educational Studies at Goldsmiths College. She is also Co-ordinator of the Goldsmiths Centre for Cross Curricular Initiatives and co-author (with Martin Buck) of *Curriculum Guidance No 1: Whole School Provision for Personal and Social Development*, 1992 and *Curriculum Guidance No 2: Re-affirming Values*, 1993. She is currently Associate Director to the HEA Promoting Health in Secondary Schools Project.

Pauline Lyseight-jones is General Inspector: Curriculum Evaluation and Assessment for the London Borough of Ealing and has worked in primary, secondary and higher education and in the voluntary education sector. Her contributions to journal and books includes a chapter in *Assessment in the Multi-ethnic Primary Classroom* (Trentham, 1994).

Paul Patrick has been teaching in London schools since 1972 and is Head of Year in a south east London Comprehensive. He was an advisory teacher for ILEA's Relationships and Sexuality Project and a member of ILEA's PSHE advisory panel. He has worked as an educational adviser on several sexuality education videos produced by ILEA and wrote and presented a set of interactive videos for KS3 PSHE. He has lectured, trained, written and broadcasted on issues of PSHE and particularly sexuality education for the past twelve years. He was a founder member of the Lesbian and Gay Teachers Group and has been an openly gay teacher since 1974.

Elizabeth Plackett is Lecturer in Education at Goldsmiths College. She worked in inner London for twenty years as an English teacher, a reading teacher and as an advisory teacher. She has a particular interest in the uses of reading in the secondary school.

Michael Young is Senior Lecturer in Sociology of Education and Head of the Post-16 Education Centre at the Institute of Education, University of London. His research interests include curriculum issues in secondary and post-secondary education and their links to technological developments and changes in world economies. He has recently acted as a consultant to OECD, has been a specialist adviser to the House of Commons Select Committee on Education and adviser to the Centre for Educational Policy and Policy Development on an integrated framework for education and training in South Africa. He is co-author of *A British Baccalaureate* (IPRR, 1990).

Introduction

This book has been written during a period of review and reassessment of the educational directions which we have been required to take during the post Education Reform Act (ERA) years. In the past year we have seen the Dearing review of the National Curriculum potentially re-opening spaces and opportunities for schools to win back some control over the curriculum. We are now in the position where schools can either hold to a view that their curriculum will remain fundamentally determined by the National Curriculum. Alternatively they can take the opportunity to re-evaluate some fundamental purposes of the curriculum and determine ways in which that curriculum can in practice promote the broad and balanced education of the whole child in a way that is coherent and relevant.

Clearly there are a number of pressures and unresolved issues. For example, there is still overload at Key Stage 2; there are uncertainties and concerns about how the 14-19 curriculum will eventually shape up; external assessment is still over- determining much curriculum practice; the standards debate continues to push schools towards selection, streaming, and narrow curriculum provision. The School Curriculum and Assessment Authority's apparent indifference to the cross-curricular dimensions, themes and skills[1] is disheartening for those concerned to retain a full curriculum entitlement as required by the ERA. At a different level, the weakening authority of local education authorities with LMS and the emergence of Grant Maintained schools has potentially reduced the significance of more local curriculum initiatives which flourished before the impact of the ERA. In addition, adequate funding to support curriculum change remains a key issue for many schools within the state system. However, in spite of these difficulties there seems to be growing evidence of a resurgence of energy and commitment around the need to review some basic curriculum principles, not just the National Curriculum. This book represents one manifestation of that new energy.

The book is concerned with the personal development of pupils within the educational process. The book's various authors share a commitment to the promotion of a coherent and relevant as well as broad and balanced curriculum. Such a curriculum must be underpinned by explicit aims and values. All would argue for pupils' personal development to be at the centre of whole curriculum planning, to be at the heart of a school's purpose and rationale. Central to personal development is a concern for equity and justice and thus all the contributors share a commitment towards an education which enables the child to find her/himself both within themselves and in relation to others; and which enables each child, through a particular relation between content and process, to develop the understandings and skills to better enable them to have the capacity to shape the world, in which they live both now and in the future.

Schools are at a crossroads — which direction should they take? This book urges them to take a direction which requires them to clarify and be explicit and confident about their shared values, to embed these values within their structures and practices and to regularly monitor and review them. It urges them to ensure that all members of the school community participate in decisions and initiatives and feel valued and respected. It urges them to move more towards becoming more critical and self-examining institutions. Institutions which believe that they can and do make a difference to the lives of their pupils. Institutions which can help to produce young adults more able to help shape their own future.

In chapter 1, we describe some of the initiatives which help to re-affirm the centrality of pupils' personal development. They draw on the work of OFSTED in the UK and that of the Scottish Consultative Council on the Curriculum in Scotland. The chapter explores some ideas for learning outcomes for personal development and offers a revised framework for planning and implementing these outcomes in a critical and coherent fashion. Chapters 2, 3 and 4 are all concerned with issues of equality and identity and how they relate to personal development. Burke reveals the extent to which equal opportunities has been devalued since the ERA and argues for the centrality of equal opportunities to the promotion of personal development and having reviewed the downplaying of equal opportunities in the late 80s and early 90s suggests that schools now have re-emerging opportunities to maintain and strengthen their EO work through initiatives such as the OFSTED requirements, quality and school effectiveness movements. She urges schools to take these opportunities and to ensure that EO is central to their whole school curriculum policy and practice.

Lyseight-jones re-examines the place of race and cultural diversity within what she calls the 'healthy development' of the individual. She poses some fundamental questions about the ways in which schools and teachers can more sensitively and effectively enable their young people to grow. She uses her discussions with primary and secondary students to suggest some areas of concern for schools: fairness, bullying, justice, name-calling and overt racist issues. Lyseight-jones warns against a simplistic approach to cultural diversity in schools, arguing for seeing black and ethnic minority children not just in terms of their past histories but also in terms of their current and future histories. She outlines a black mentoring scheme which attempts to focus on self-esteem and achievement as one way of addressing some of the concerns she raises.

Hanson and Patrick take sexuality education as the focus for their chapter. They take the reader through the contradictions at policy level which result from the requirements for health education targets which explicitly encompass sexual education with an idealogically-driven concern for a very limited sex education in the name of individual freedom, parental rights and a one dimensional morality. Hanson and Patrick demonstrate that even in an era dominated by reductionist notions of sex education there are still clear opportunities to initiate and sustain whole school policies and practices for sexual education which 'provides young people with an understanding of their sexuality, the choices which flow from it and the knowledge, understandings and power to make those choices positive, responsible and informed'.

Chapters 5, 6 and 7 explore particular aspects or features of personal development: citizenship, literacy and spiritual and moral development. In chapter 5, we re-examine education, for citizenship within the current curriculum constraints and opportunities, arguing for a broad, maximalist version of citizenship education radical in perspective and underpinning all aspects of the school's work. This model is then developed within the taught curriculum through two case studies of curriculum planning drawn from the primary phase — case studies of planning the topics of 'Ourselves' and 'Food and Sustainability' are described using the personal development framework outlined in chapter 1. Chapter 6 takes literacy as a key element of schooling and describes how it is often viewed almost as a technical skill rather than as something which is central to personal growth and identity and crucial to the empowerment of young people. Plackett shows us how literacy relates to young peoples' futures not just as workers but as future citizen. She argues that a school which recognises this model of literacy will need to adopt a range of agreed whole-school strategies which promote literacy across all curriculum areas and make the development of literacy a central responsibility of all members of the school community. She outlines what some of these whole-school strategies might be at secondary level. Broadbent in chapter 7 explores the spiritual and moral aspects of pupils' personal development. She clarifies and extends the too often narrow meanings of these dimensions of our lives and links them to other aspects of personal development. Broadbent shows with some vivid examples how these complex understandings, skills and attitudes around culture, belief, morality and identity can be fruitfully planned for across a range of curriculum areas from a very young age.

Chapter 8 takes us into a discussion of the future, educating for the 21st century. Hicks argues for a citizenship education which enables us and our pupils to 'set the concerns in their global context and ......relate the issues of today to the needs of future generations.' He demonstrates how and why a citizenship education which fails to work with issues around where we are going and where we want to go will also fail to empower young people, will prevent them from developing the skills and qualities which would enable them to make choices about their future. Hicks outlines some useful activities and strategies to help children to develop a futures perspective are outlined.

Chapter 9 considers the 14-19 curriculum. Young begins by underlining the message of this book — that schools need to define their curriculum purposes and ensure that curriculum areas are developed in relation to the overall purposes of the school. He uses 'connective integration' as a curriculum model based on educational purpose and contrasts it with the 'bureaucratic integration' model still dominant in many secondary schools, in which the curriculum is organised around relatively autonomous subjects. Young suggests that in England the curriculum still assumes that young people have completed their personal development by 16 and argues for a coherent curriculum framework in which students' personal development is central. He points out that global economic changes are requiring employees with the knowledge, skills and values associated with personal development — in other words, that personal development is increasingly central to employability.

This book explores the directions in which schools are going. It urges schools and teachers to stand back and reflect on some fundamental purposes of education and to hold on to the principles of 'broad, balanced and relevant' enshrined in the 1988 Act so that their curriculum extends beyond the National Curriculum. Schools can and do make a difference to our pupils' lives — the kind of difference schools can make is largely up to us.

Notes

1. See Whitty G, Rowe and G, Anggleton P, *Subjects and Themes in the Secondary School Curriculum Research Papers in Education Vol 9, No. 2, 1994* for a full discussion of the marginalisation of the cross-curricular themes within the school curriculum.

Chapter One

Setting a framework for personal development

Martin Buck and Sally Inman

Our introduction briefly traced the emergence of provision for pupils' personal development as a central thread of several national initiatives since the 1988 ERA. This chapter uses the context of such initiatives to provide a more detailed discussion about what is meant by pupils' personal development, with particular emphasis on personal development outcomes. We also present the reader with a framework by which to make sense of personal development and which may help teachers to plan and structure whole curriculum provision for the personal development of their pupils in a more effective fashion.

Preparing for the future

The personal development of young people does not take place in a social vacuum but within a particular set of social arrangements including families, communities and nations. Young people will also become adults within a particular and possibly very different set of social arrangements. Central to our understanding of pupils' personal development, then, must be the clarification of the present society in which pupils live and the nature of the future society in which young people will be adults, for both will require of its members the skills and qualities needed of citizens.

What kind of future are we preparing our young people for?

There is no one accepted version of the future, since what we know about the future is in some part predicated upon what we wish that future to be. There are therefore different and competing futures. Whilst we can predict some of the requirements of our future citizens in terms of what we know about the changing patterns of technology, industry, employment, leisure and life styles — though this is open to interpretation — the nature of that future will also in part depend on the young people themselves, their hopes and the possibilities they perceive for alternative futures. These hopes and possibilities will in turn be partially influenced by the nature of the personal development we promote and foster in schools. Thus as educators we need both a vision of what the future might be like but also what we would like that future to be, for the latter will inform the sorts of skills and qualities we attempt to foster in our future adults. This is not to be naive or idealist, for we recognise that schools may have a relatively small impact on pupils' lives. That impact can, however, be a significant one. In the words of Robin Richardson (1992):

> Schools are not powerless; they are not doomed to be mere victims or pawns, nor bound merely to breed dependency and passivity amongst their pupils.

So what do we know about the future? Accepting the qualifications in the previous paragraph there is nevertheless increasing consensus about some features of the 21st century. There is, for example, increasing agreement that the post-industrial 21st century society will be one which will require a very different workforce; one that will need to be both flexible and highly skilled so as to manage and control the expected rates of technological development and to be able to sustain levels of economic development. That society may also be one in which the survival of the whole planet may be at stake unless its citizens act with responsibility and self-restraint. It is likely to be one in which citizens are more obviously citizens of the world as the interdependence of all nations becomes ever more real.

So we can begin to identify the particular knowledge, skills and attributes which may be required of citizens of the future. However, we should also attempt to spell out our vision of the sort of society we would want for our young people: the economic, cultural, social and moral framework by which we should want future citizens to live. For it is this vision which will also help to determine the conception of personal development which we wish to promote through education and elsewhere. There have been a number of attempts at producing visions of the future. In the 60s and 70s a number of educators produced visions of the future. The writing of educators such as Freire, Illich, Kohl and others were all in their very different ways critiques of the current society and educational systems. They were also attempts to use education to transform the present society, to move towards a new future. The 80s and 90s have been less 'visionary', for reasons which lay largely outside the educational arena but are located within the wider political and economic structures. Nevertheless there have been some significant attempts to outline possible futures. Since David Hicks in his chapter looks in depth at futures education, we will limit ourselves here to a few brief references to work in this important area.

Visions of the future — a more sustainable society

One vision of how human beings might, and indeed should, live with each other and with the non-human world appears in Selby, 1995. From a concern for how we currently relate to each other and to the non-human world an ethical framework for how this could be different is outlined. The framework is described as 'elements of a world ethic for living sustainably' and suggests the values, moral codes and rights which should underpin this new way of living. These elements are outlined in figure 1.

The elements provide a vision of a society in which diversity is positively embraced; in which there is equality between human beings and between human beings and the non-human world; and in which human beings have clearly defined rights but also have responsibilities towards each other and towards nature. *Caring for the Earth* (1991) sets out a set of core democratic values — the values by which people should live:

- respect for reasoning
- respect for truth
- fairness
- acceptance of diversity
- co-operation

Figure 1

- every human being is part of the community of life. This community embraces cultural and natural diversity.

- every human being has the same fundamental and equal rights

- each person and each society is entitled to respect of these rights and is responsible for the protection of these rights for others

- every life form warrants respect independently of its worth to people

- everyone should take responsibility for her/his impacts on nature

- everyone should aim to share fairly the benefits and costs of resource use

- each generation should leave to the future a world at least as diverse and productive as the one it inherited

- the protection of human rights and those of the rest of nature is a world-wide responsibility. The responsibility is both individual and collective

- justice
- freedom
- equality
- concern for welfare of others
- peaceful resolution of conflict

These, then, are the ethical and moral codes and the core values which should be enshrined in a future society. The vision clearly embraces a radical conception of a society very different than those we know. The vision also suggests that there are imperatives to move towards this form of society if the human species is to have a diverse and productive future.

Visions of the future — a more knowledgeable, skilled, successful and collaborative society?

Sally Tomlinson, in an article in the *Times Educational Supplement* of August 1993, discusses her vision of the future society, outlining the skills, knowledge and values which she believes will be required of its members. She says:

> In the society of the future all young people will need to be able to solve problems, (including some yet not imagined) to think for themselves, to engage in life-time learning, to work in co-operation with others and to participate in the knowledge society which has long been forecast, and is now upon us.

The attributes Tomlinson identifies can be fostered and developed through education. The National Commission on Education, in its report of 1993, takes a similar view, arguing that large numbers of workers with knowledge and what they call applied intelligence, will be crucial to the future economic success of Britain. The wider purposes of education should, the commission believes, promote patterns of 'learning to succeed' in children:

> It is central to our vision for education in the next century that all children should from a very early age learn to succeed and go on succeeding.

Figure 2: The Commission's Vision

1. In all countries knowledge and applied intelligence have become central to economic success and personal and social well-being.

2. In the United Kingdom much higher achievement in education and training is needed to match world standards.

3. Everyone must want to learn and to have ample opportunity and encouragement to do so.

4. All children must achieve a good grasp of literacy and basic skills early on as the foundation for learning throughout life.

5. The full range of people's abilities must be recognised and their development rewarded.

6. High quality learning depends above all on the knowledge, skill, effort and example of teachers and trainers.

7. It is the role of education both to interpret and pass on the values of society and to stimulate people to think for themselves and to change the world around them.

The Commission describes 'our vision for the future'. The kind of education and training which they believe will be needed to produce involved and effective citizens in the next century. Figure 2 shows the Commission's vision.

Thus a number of people and organisations have attempted to provide a vision of the future and outlined some of the attributes required of future citizens. Clearly all such visions have implications for the kind of education we provide for our future citizens — they suggest particular learning and personal development outcomes which young people will need if they are to be able to understand and 'manage' the present and to promote and sustain a different future. It is to these personal development outcomes which we now turn.

Personal development — outcomes

In *Curriculum Guidance No 1*, we suggested that teachers, particularly in England and Wales, did not have useful guidance on what might constitute the personal and social development of pupils. We observed that, for example, National Curriculum Council (NCC) guidance as provided in NCC Curriculum Guidance 3 and Circular 6 is open to very different and possibly conflicting meanings and often 'glosses over' important issues and offered our own conception of personal and social development. We advocated a focus on both the *processes* of personal and social development and the *outcomes* of these processes: 'any conception of personal and social development must involve an explicit statement as to the kinds of adults we wish our young people to become and also outline the appropriate knowledge, skills and understandings and the necessary learning experiences that will enable them to achieve this outcome'. We outlined the outcomes we would wish to see in young people — the attributes we would want them to have as adults. Since then we have modified and expanded this list in light of our work with teachers. The personal development outcomes we now suggest are as follows:

- to have high self-esteem
- to be confident and assertive
- to be self-aware; knowledgeable about themselves
- to be able to take responsibility for their own actions and the effects of these actions on others

Figure 3

High self-esteem — concerned with how we see ourselves. It suggests a capacity to grow as individuals who have confidence in our relationships with others and are able to sustain confidence in the self without constant affirmation from those around us.

Being confident and assertive partly an outcome of high self-esteem, it requires self-knowledge and an ability to reflect on one's own attitudes and values. Being confident and assertive involves being able to articulate our values and beliefs through our relationships with others.

Being self-aware and knowledgeable requires an understanding of one's own attitudes and values and where they come from ie. what and who has shaped who we are. It includes an understanding of the formation of gender and sexuality within specific cultural patterns. It suggests a capacity to engage in self-reflection and also a capacity for change.

Being able to maintain effective interpersonal relationships within a moral framework suggests a degree of independence and autonomy, together with an appropriate need and desire for others. It requires self-knowledge and an awareness of the differing values and attitudes of others. It implies a capacity to make decisions within our own value system.

Being able to take responsibility for own actions and the effects of these actions upon others — implies self-knowledge and a developed value system. It also requires empathy.

Understanding and, where appropriate, being sensitive to the beliefs, values and ways of life of others — suggests that understanding requires empathy as well as knowledge and analytical skills. It requires us to develop sensitivity to others' values, but set within the context of our own value system.

Figure 3 (continued)

Being critically informed about the human and physical world — requires an understanding of interdependent, interpersonal, local, national and global issues. It suggests an ability to ask the questions 'who, what, why and when' about such issues.

Being able to question taken for granted assumptions and beliefs — requires an ability to ask the questions outlined in the previous outcome. Implies self-knowledge so we can question our own assumptions.

Being able to think critically — implies the development of logical and rational thinking within a value system. It requires the ability to interpret, analyse, synthesise and evaluate.

Being concerned about promoting justice on an interpersonal, societal and global scale implies a developed value system within which the promotion of justice and equality are seen as central to our humanity. It requires knowledge, understanding and commitment to democratic values.

Promoting a concern for all forms of life, now and in the future — implies values which support a sustainable way of life. It requires an understanding of the interdependence of all forms of life on the planet, realising the effects of our behaviour on the non-human world, other people and future generations.

Being skilled in how to work collaboratively Collaboration requires participants who are skilled individual learners, able to take responsibility and make decisions. They require the values and skills which promote sharing and equality. It suggests that collaboration is central to effective social change.

Capacity to reflect on own learning and plan for future developments — requires self-knowledge and reflection, decision making and planning skills, appropriate goal-setting and an ability to evaluate.

- to be able to maintain effective interpersonal relationships within a moral framework
- to be able to understand and, where appropriate, be sensitive to and respect the beliefs, values and ways of life of others
- to be critically informed about the human and physical world
- to be able to question taken for granted assumptions and beliefs
- to be able to think critically
- to be concerned about promoting fairness, justice and equality on an interpersonal, societal and global level
- to be able to promote a concern for all forms of life, now and in the future
- to be skilled in how to work collaboratively and autonomously
- to be able to reflect on their learning and plan for future developments.

This is not a definitive list of personal and social development outcomes but rather an attempt to pin-point some of the critical attributes which we believe we should be promoting in our young people. In *Curriculum Guidance No 2* we attempted to break down each of the outcomes so as to inform teachers about them in greater detail. An amended version of this is shown in Fig 3.

In *Curriculum Guidance No.1* (CG1) we argued for a conception of personal and social development in which the constant interplay between the personal and the social is present. As we said then, and believe still:

> ....personal growth, involving increasing self awareness, self esteem, and confidence is a complex and often painful process which requires an understanding of the immediate, societal and global contexts in which the individual is located. In other words, personal growth always has a critical and social dimension.

Thus we have been concerned with a conception of personal development which provides us with a particular set of outcomes — ones which we believe describe some of the qualities young people will need if they are to be able to forge a more democratic and sustainable future.

Other initiatives: OFSTED

Since our *Curriculum Guidance* books were published, there has been a whole series of initiatives focusing on outcomes and attempting to define more precisely the kinds of personal qualities and attitudes we might want to foster in our young people. In *CG2* we discussed some of the more recent National Curriculum Council initiatives, particularly the NCC March 1993 paper on Spiritual and Moral development. We also reviewed the OFSTED National Inspection Framework. Since *CG2*, the inspection framework has once again been revised, this time providing more guidance on how to define and evaluate spiritual, moral, social and personal development.

OFSTED has also begun to explore critical issues around values and personal development in some depth. In their March 1994 discussion paper on spiritual, moral, social and cultural development OFSTED seeks to provide guidance on how we might understand and define each of these critical areas of personal development and formulate outcomes for each. This seems a major step forward from the somewhat vague and sometimes ambiguous statements about personal development which have been offered by HMI in the past. The discussion paper begins by acknowledging the difficulties in defining personal development, accepting that 'personal development is not easily susceptible to evaluation of quality or standards on a five point scale.' Also that such development is not 'necessarily smooth or continuous'; that individuals develop at different rates and in different ways; that changes may be difficult to detect; that measurement is difficult; that it is not always easy to separate what the school as opposed to other forces such as home or community have contributed to a pupil's personal development. They recognise that a wealth of personal and societal factors will affect each individual's personal development — thus factors such as gender and ethnicity are put alongside more 'individual' factors such as age and personality.

The 1994 paper focuses on what outcomes we could expect for the four areas of personal development. It sets out to specify what attributes and qualities are associated with persons who are spiritually, morally, socially and culturally developed. The suggested outcomes for each area are shown in Fig 4.

Figure 4 OFSTED 1994 Discussion Paper

Spiritual Development
• knowledge of the central beliefs, ideas and practices of major world religions and philosophies
• an understanding of how people have sought to explain the universe through various myths and stories, including religious, historical and scientific interpretations
• beliefs which are held personally, and the ability to give some account of these and to derive values from them
• behaviour and attitudes which derive from such knowledge and understanding and from personal conviction, and which show awareness of the relationship between belief and action
• personal response to guest ions about the purpose of life, and to the experience of e.g. beauty and love or pain and suffering

Moral Development
• knowledge of the language and ideas of morality and, increasingly, how these differ from e.g. legal or political usage or from other kinds of statement (logical or factual)
• understanding of the nature and purpose of moral discussion, with the desire to persuade combined with respect for, and listening to, others viewpoints
• personal values in relation to:
the self (awareness, confidence, esteem, control, reliance, respect, discipline, responsibility) relationships with others (tolerance, respect for persons and property, truthfulness, compassion, co-operativeness, sensitivity, love)
local, national and world issues (individual and the community -
rights, duties and responsibilities, war and peace, human rights, exploitation and aid, medical ethics, environmental issues, equal opportunities)
• the disposition to act and behave in accordance with such values, including the skills of making moral decisions and forming moral judgements

Social Development
• knowledge of the ways in which societies function or are organised —
rom the family to the school and thence to wider groupings
• understanding of how individuals relate to each other and to the institutions, structures and processes of society, and how what is learnt in the curriculum relates to life in society
• attitudes which show the capacity to adjust to a range of social contexts by appropriate and sensitive behaviour
• skills in taking on the roles of leader and team worker exercising responsibility, initiative, and co-operation
• ability to make a strong personal contribution to the well being of social groups and to for4 effective relationships within them

Cultural Development
• knowledge of the nature and roots of their own cultural traditions and practices and the key features of other major cultural groups within their own society
• understanding of the diversity of religious, social, aesthetic, ethnic and political traditions and practices — nationally and internationally
• personal response and accomplishment in a range of cultural fields
• capacity to relate what they learn, in school generally and in particular areas of the curriculum, to their appreciation of wider cultural aspects of society, and to evaluate the quality and worth of cultural achievements

A closer look at these outcomes would suggest that many of the skills, attitudes etc, are ones which we would subscribe to and which we have listed ourselves in this and earlier publications. There is, however, a problem in dividing personal development up in this way — do the four aspects add up to the whole person? Is personal development adequately covered by 'spiritual, moral, social and cultural' or are there other aspects, such as emotional and physical and intellectual development. Schools will need to ask themselves whether the SMSC formula covers all aspects of their pupils' personal development. Is their pupils' emotional development adequately covered by the outcomes mentioned under the formula — the attributes of sensitivity, love, compassion, for example, which are listed under moral development. If not, schools may need to review their own personal development outcomes, including the emotional, and relate theirs to the OFSTED list, rather than starting from the OFSTED list. Part of the problem lies in starting with the parts and moving to the whole: there are serious questions about whether you can ever achieve a holistic approach if you work in this way. However, despite these caveats we would want to applaud HMI for engaging in such a difficult task and would see this discussion paper as a significant contribution to the emerging debate around pupils' personal development.

There is not space here to look in detail at all four personal development categories explored in the OFSTED paper. We have therefore limited ourselves to a brief discussion of one — moral development. We have chosen this aspect as it is one area of personal development which very obviously relates to our own work on personal development outcomes and makes explicit references to the terrain of the cross-curricular themes and dimensions.

Moral development — outcomes

OFSTED suggests that pupils give evidence of moral behaviour if they display:

- knowledge of the language and ideas of morality
- understanding of the nature and purpose of moral discussion
- personal values in relation to:

  the self (self-awareness; self-confidence; self-esteem; self-control; self-reliance; self-respect; self-discipline; responsibility) relationships with others (tolerance; respect for persons and property; truthfulness; compassion; co-operativeness; sensitivity; love)

local, national and world issues (with reference to such issues as: individual and the community — rights, duties, and responsibilities; war and peace; human rights; exploitation and aid; medical ethics; environmental issues; equal opportunities)

We can see that for HMI moral development explicitly embraces the development of pupils' knowledge and understanding as well as attitudes and values; it demonstrates the interplay between the personal and the social, including the global and points directly to areas of exploration and understanding around health, the environment, citizenship and education for international understanding — the cross-curricular themes. Moral development, as described here, would also seem to point to personal values of the kind which embrace equal opportunities and multicultural perspectives.

Other initiatives: the Scottish example

The Scottish Consultative Council on the Curriculum in for example *Values in Education* (1991) has outlined the values that it wishes to promote through education. The document outlines five main areas: appreciation of learning; respect and caring for self; respect and caring for others; a sense of belonging and social responsibility. Within each area there is an attempt to spell out the particular values education should promote in young people — as shown in Fig 5. In 1993 the Scottish Office Education Department published National guidelines for personal and social development from 5-14. These guidelines (see Fig. 5) set out the aims of personal development as to help pupils to:

- have an appropriately positive regard for self, and for others and their needs
- develop the life skills to enable them to participate effectively and safely in society
- identify, review and evaluate the values they and society hold and recognise that these affect thoughts and actions.
- take increasing responsibility for their own lives.

Figure 5. from Scottish Consultative Council on the Curriculum (1991)

Appreciation of Learning
The Council is committed to help learners to develop an appreciation of learning which includes:
• a commitment to learning as a life-long activity
• a developing understanding of the nature of knowledge and how it is constructed and used
• self-discipline, independent thinking, aesthetic sensitivity
• the development of skills which help individual pupils to reach their full potential
• a developing understanding of theimportance of a cultural perspective, respect for evidence and freedom of expression as foundation elements of a democratic society

Respect and Caring for Self
The SCCC is committed to help learners to develop respect and caring for self which includes:
• self-esteem and a feeling of self-confidence
• an accurate assessment of personal strengths
• responsibility for self
• the ability and drive to develop towards full human potential

Respect and Caring for Others
The SCCC is committed to help learners to develop respect and caring for others which includes:
• recognising that every person is a unique and worthwhile individual
• valuing racial, ethnic and religious diversity
• learning and appreciating the skills and sensitivities through which respect and care are expressed

A Sense of Belonging
The SCCC is committed to assisting learners at school, their parents and guardians to a recognition that they are valued, contributing members of a caring educational community. In addition, it seeks to promote recognition that pupils in school belong to a variety of caring communities which include:
• families, which are generally the first communities children experience and which are the foundation of the child's sense of belonging
• religious and cultural communities which also have a profound influence on many children
• the local community
• the wider communities of Scotland, the United Kingdom, Europe and the World

Social Responsibility
The SCCC is committed to develop among all learners personal responsibility in society at local, national and international levels. This includes:
• developing skills and attitudes which enable citizens to contribute to the process by which every society continues to clarify, review and improve its own values
• respecting democratic processes by which differences of opinions are resolved non-violently within society
• respecting justice
• respecting and caring for the environment
• appreciating the ways in which wealth is generated and the impact of wealth creation on the world community and on the environment
• developing ways whereby individuals and groups can contribute to the well-being of the world community

Figure 6. Scottish Office (1993)

Appendix

All examples have been collated here to provide an overview which should be useful to teachers in their planning.

EXAMPLES OF PUPILS' POTENTIAL DEVELOPMENT

Self-Awareness

Know themselves as unique individuals;

acknowledge aptitudes and abilities;

understand that they are continually developing and changing;.

recognise and express moods and feelings.

Identify their own values and attitudes;

begin to have views of their own aptitudes and abilities;

search for evidence about personal performance;

begin to recognise a range of emotions and how they deal with them.

Have developing attitudes of self-respect through critical appreciation of self;

begin to make a realistic assessment of their abiiities and aptitudes;

recognise that developing self-awareness may lead to an increase in self control.

Self Esteem

Express positive thoughts about themselves and their abilities;

cope with everyday situations;

cope with moderate degrees of change.

Be positive about themselves and their social and cultural backgrounds;

demonstrate the confidence to tackle situations that they find unfamiliar;

approach new challenges and difficulties with confidence;

recognise that their perception of self is affected by responses from others.

Understand the importance of valuing self;

demonstrate enterprise and initiative in appropriate situations;

recognise that making mistakes can provide opportunities for learning;

have the confidence to retain a reasoned position.

The guidelines also spell out some outcomes for personal and social development. Personal development is seen as essentially concerned with two major areas: self-awareness and self-esteem.

Similarly social development is seen as concerned with two major areas: inter-personal relationships and independence and inter-dependence.

The guidelines go on to outline some more specific outcomes for each of these areas and to specify the appropriate learning contexts which will help to develop the outcomes. An example of how this is achieved for one of these areas is given in Fig 6.

Finally, the guidelines provide some suggestions for appropriate ways of assessing, recording and reporting personal and social development.

Here we see an initiative which, like the OFSTED paper, takes personal development seriously, acknowledging the complexities in defining and measuring this aspect of pupils' development but also being prepared to offer some starting points. The similarities between many of the outcomes described in the Scottish guidelines with those which we have been working on in our *Curriculum Guidance* publications and those outlined by OFSTED suggests a growing consensus on how we might define and measure the personal development of our pupils' future. We applaud Scotland's initiative, attempting to spell out personal development outcomes — the very attempt to specify how values can be at the centre of the curriculum is an important achievement, one not made by the NCC nor by the School Curriculum and Assessment Authority (SCAA). The guidelines from the Scottish Office are as important for what they say about educational priorities in Scottish education as they are for the specific conception of personal development which they are operating.

There is, we believe, a re-emerging interest in personal development in some quarters of educational thinking and policy making. However, we need to set this interest in the context of earlier concern for pupils' personal development, as demonstrated through curriculum debate and guidance around the cross-curricular themes, skills and dimensions.

Personal development and the cross-curricular elements

We suggested in our introduction that the post-Dearing curriculum will be inadequate unless and until it is underpinned by an explicit and agreed set of values and we noted the official silence over the place of

17

cross-curricular themes within the new slimmed down curriculum in England and Wales. In view of this silence, teachers may wish to ask themselves how young people can become personally and socially developed without reference to the exploration of matters such as:

- health issues at a personal, community, national and global level. This would embrace the generic skills, values and attitude formation such as decision-making and self-esteem as well as more specific concerns such as sexual health and drugs education

- the range of economic decision-making processes and practices which affect our daily lives and how these are determined

- the major ecological issues facing the planet and our individual responsibilities regarding them

- the knowledge and skills involved in understanding, and being able to practice, the rights and responsibilities associated with being a citizen.

Teachers should also ask themselves whether the cross-curricular skills of, for example, communication, study, numeracy and literacy are sufficiently and effectively embedded within subjects as revised through the new national curriculum. The cross-curricular dimensions remain critical to any curriculum which claims to be concerned with pupils' personal development. In *CG2* we argued that ' without these dimensions (specifically equal opportunities and multicultural education) the personal and social development of young people will be denied'. It seems inconceivable that we could create a curriculum in which personal development was central without an explicit commitment to these critical strands of our experience.

We are now in the unfortunate position where curriculum reduction — in the name of manageability and avoidance of overload — and what has been described as returning autonomy to teachers, has in effect made the gap between the aims of the ERA and the subject- based curriculum wider than ever. The original National Curriculum was weak from the outset in this respect, in that there was never a real understanding of a whole curriculum perspective which put personal development at the centre. However, despite the bolt-on nature of the cross-curricular elements, the fact that they were the subject of NCC curriculum guidance and, latterly, of early versions of the OFSTED framework, suggested that the elements were to be taken seriously and were pivotal to provision for personal development. Now, in spite of Dearing's acknowledgement of the need for education to 'not be concerned only with equipping students with the knowledge and skills they need to earn a living' but to: 'help our young people to use leisure time creatively; have respect for other people, other cultures and other beliefs; become good citizens; think things out for themselves; pursue a healthy life-style; and, not least, value themselves and their achievements...' (1993) the reality of that challenge is to be found only within the small references to sex education and careers education and guidance.

The post-Dearing curriculum is likely to be more, rather than less, fragmented. There seems to be no framework on which to hang its constituent parts. Yet the need for such a framework has, if anything, increased. What follows is one attempt to provide one such a framework, in the hope that it makes a contribution to continuing discussion concerning the provision for pupils' personal development within schools.

A framework for personal development

In *CG1* we outlined a framework for planning the curriculum provision for the personal and social development of pupils and sought particularly to provide a way of interrelating the different cross-curricular elements and to provide coherence across the five themes. This framework consisted of a set of central questions which we believed to be at the very heart of pupils' personal development. Each of the nine questions was supported by organising ideas and concepts. The organising ideas provided contexts in which the questions could be explored, to ensure that the interconnections between the personal and the social are built in and also the socio-spacial scale of family, community, societal and global. As the building blocks needed to span the five themes, concepts such as power, justice, rights, freedom were described — concepts which can be used to make sense of a whole range of apparently disparate areas of our experience. We also tried to show how the nine questions, together with their organising ideas and concepts, could be used to 'cover' the substance of the NCC guidance for the themes, albeit in a more interrelated way.

Since we first outlined this framework in 1992 we have become aware of a number of weaknesses in the original design:

- The nine questions do not cover all the important concerns which we would wish pupils to explore as part of their personal development, in particular its inadequacy to deal with sustainability. We have, largely through the work of OFSTED, become aware of the limited extent to which the framework can deal with purpose and meaning — an important spiritual and philosophical dimension was missing.

- The organising ideas have always been problematic both for us and for teachers. Teachers have tended to deal with this by ignoring the organising ideas and defining the framework solely in terms of the central questions. The reason for this seems to lie with the nature of the organising ideas as they were originally expressed — they added to the planning process in a way not always understood by teachers. However, without the organising ideas the breadth and balance of the framework as a planning tool was considerably weakened.

- The framework was underpinned by a model of teaching and learning — one which promoted participative and collaborative approaches in which the development of skills was critical. However, in *CG1* this model was not explicitly described, so the framework could be seen as over-intellectual, concerned only with pupils' cognitive development. In *CG2* we attempted to demonstrate how the framework worked as a planning tool in which the promotion of experiential and participative learning was critical. The chapters by David Scott and Helena Burke in *CG2* described this process in some detail.

- The phrasing of some of the questions and organising ideas at times reflected our past work and concerns. Too often they reflected a sociological perspective, over-concerned with societal structures and institutions at the expense of the personal and interpersonal and we ignored our own stated perspective — to have a constant interplay between the personal and the social.

The revised framework

The revised framework outlined below has been modified to try to take account of some of these weaknesses.

i.   The questions have been increased to eleven in order to improve the framework. The additional questions reflect ongoing discussions with teachers and LEA advisers when piloting the original framework. They also reflect our attempt to embrace the work of HMI in the OFSTED discussion paper referred to earlier.

ii. Some of the central questions have been adapted, to make their meaning clearer or to shift the emphasis of the question. For example, the question: 'In what ways are people different and with what consequences?' now reads: 'On what bases do people categorise others?' This change reflects our concern that the original question could be open to undesired interpretations, for example, as implying a natural difference between people as opposed to structural arrangements which bring about differences. The question: 'How do people learn the requirements of a particular culture?' has now become: 'How do we acquire our social identities?' to elicit a less deterministic and more open position with regard to patterns of socialisation.

iii. The organising ideas have been turned into what we now describe as organising questions. We hope that we have thus made the ideas more accessible and more clearly related to the outcomes we wish to promote and to the categories of spiritual, moral, social and cultural development with which OFSTED are concerned.

The central questions remain philosphical in nature and become concretised through their application to a range of different contexts indicated through the organising questions. The central questions overlap and cut across different parts of our lives. Their overlapping reflects how we experience the world.

What can the framework offer? How does it help teachers to:

- Meet the requirements of the ERA — that is, plan explicit provision for pupils' personal development and make their education a preparation for their future lives?

- Meet the requirements of the OFSTED Inspection Framework, particularly in relation to Section 5.1 which deals with the personal development of pupils?

We are convinced that the framework has a contribution to make in this area. It can help us to develop whole school policies and practices with regard to personal development. In terms of the taught curriculum it can help us to plan for explicit learning opportunities to foster the knowledge, skills and attitudes associated with the spiritual, moral, social and cultural development of pupils.

The eleven questions are as follows:

1. **What is the nature of our rights and responsibilities in everyday life?**
   This question explores individuals rights and responsibilities as members of families, as employers and employees, as consumers and as citizens of a particular country and of the world.

2. **On what bases do people influence and control others?**
   This question explores the different ways people have power and authority. For example, through work, religious practice, politics. It looks at people's ability to make decisions and how these decisions affect their own lives and the lives of others.

3. **What is the balance between individual freedom and the constraints necessary for co-operative living?**
   This question explores some of the consequences which arise from the choices people make for themselves and for others. For example, the consequences of different economic and political policies for people's work, leisure, health etc.

4. **In what ways do people co-operate and seek to resolve conflict?**
   This question explores relationships between people and between countries. It looks at how and why conflict or co-operation between people can operate within domestic situations, within community affairs and in international relations.

5. **On what bases do people categorise others?**
    This question explores how differences and inequalities between people, groups and nations can be reinforced or reduced by our attitudes, ideas and actions.

6. **How do we acquire our social identities?**
    This question explores how we learn attitudes, beliefs and values through our families, the media, education and the wider culture(s) in which we live.

7. **What constitutes a community; how are communities organised?**
    This question explores how communities are made up of people and the built and natural environment. It looks at the decisions made within communities, for example, about employment, homes, leisure and health provision.

8. **In what ways are the welfare of individuals and societies maintained?**
    This question explores how physical and mental health, the quality of the environment, income and wealth together make up people's welfare. It looks at the responsibilities people have for their own welfare and for the welfare of others.

9. **On what basis do people make decisions when faced with particular choices?**
    This question explores how people make choices about their family lives, their work, in buying goods and services, in their leisure activities. It looks at the effects of the choices made — for the individual, for others, and on the environment.

10. **What is our relationship to the non-human world?**
    This question explores the different attitudes human beings hold towards the physical and non-human world. It looks at the impact of human decisions and actions on the physical environment and explores notions of a sustainable society.

11. **In what ways have people sought to explain the universe and give meaning to their lives?**
    This question explores the different ways in which human beings attempt to explain the construction of the universe and their place and purpose within it.

Each of the central questions is then broken down into what we have called organising questions and the relevant concepts are identified. Thus:

Question 1: What is the nature of our rights and responsibilities in everyday life?

What kinds of rights should people have in relation to others?

What responsibilities do we have for others and for the non-human world?

How and by whom are our rights and responsibilities determined?

What responsibilities do local, national and global organisations have for people and for the non-human world?

How are our rights and responsibilities affected by things such as our age, gender, race, culture, status, material circumstances?

What rights and responsibilities do we have in different areas of our lives — eg. as parents/carers, employees/employers, citizens, consumers?

How have the rights and responsibilities of particular social groups changed over time eg children, parents, employee/employers?

How are rights and responsibilities influenced by religious beliefs and practices and by moral codes?

How do ideas about rights and responsibilities differ between societies?

Concepts: rights, responsibility, equality, inequality, interdependence, fairness, justice

Question 2: On what bases do people influence and control others?

How are we influenced by other people?

How do images and ideas from the media influence our thinking and behaviour?

How do our ideas and beliefs about power and authority affect our behaviour?

What kinds of people have influence and authority over us at different stages and parts of our lives?

In what ways do some people have power over others?

What kinds of power do groups and institutions have over individuals eg. churches, the law, police, governments?

What kinds of power do nations have over other nations?

How is our access to power and authority influenced by things such as our gender, race, economic circumstances, able- bodiedness, religion and/or religious beliefs?

How do we make sense of and give meaning to the exercise of power and authority over us?

In what ways do we resist the authority and power of others?

Concepts: power, authority, interdependence, justice

Questions 3: What is the balance between individual freedom and the constraints necessary for co-operative living?

What choices should we be free to make in different areas of our lives?

What constraints upon our actions should we accept?

How should we take account of the needs and rights of others in making choices about eg. education, transport, travel, employment, our life-styles?

How should we take account of the needs of the non-human world in making choices?

What role should morality, law, religion and government play in ensuring a balance between our individual freedom and the rights of others?

What range of views are held by governments, political parties and pressure groups about how to best preserve the freedom of individuals and satisfy the needs of society?

Concepts: freedom, constraint, rights, responsibility, welfare, health, justice, fairness

Questions 4: In what ways do people co-operate and seek to resolve conflict?

What different kinds of social relationships do people have with each other?

How are our relationships with others influenced by our own values and beliefs?

How and why do people co-operate with each other?

In what ways can and do nations co-operate with other?

What kinds of conflict can arise between people, eg. at home, at work, in the community?

What kinds of conflict can arise between social groups and between nations?

How is conflict influenced by differences and inequalities of culture, race, gender, religion, economic resources?

How can we resolve conflict between people, groups and nations?

Concepts: conflict, co-operation, culture, belief, equality, inequality, interdependence, technology

Question 5: On what bases do people categorise others?

In what ways are people similar?

In what ways are they different?

On what bases do we categorise other people and social groups?

What effects do other people's views of us have on how we see and feel about ourselves?

In what ways can differences between people lead to inequalities and discrimination?

What kinds of inequalities exist between individuals?

In what ways do people justify their unequal treatment of others?

What kinds of inequalities exist between social groups and between nations?

How can inequalities between people, groups and nations be affected by the decisions of governments and non-government organisations eg. multinational companies, aid agencies?

In what ways do people try to achieve more equality between individuals and between groups and nations?

Concepts: social differentiation, equality, colonialism, imperialism, wealth, race, gender, scarcity, justice, fairness

Question 6: How do we acquire our social identities?

In what ways, and why, do things like our gender, race, religion, influence who we are and how others see us?

How do we acquire our beliefs and values?

How and why do we sometimes change our beliefs and values during our lives?

How are we socialised into different areas and phases of our lives, eg. as children, parents, employees or employers, older people?

How do we acquire our wider cultural, political and national identities?

How do different cultures give rise to different ways of thinking and behaving?

In what ways, and why, have certain cultures become associated with influence, power and status?

Concepts: socialisation, identity, self, culture, belief, morality, equality, inequality, power, justice, fairness

Question 7: What constitutes a community; how are communities organised?

What is a community? What makes up a community?

What forms can communities take?

What do individuals need and want from their communities?

In what ways are people within a community interdependent?

In what ways are different communities interdependent?

What kinds of things do communities have to make decisions about?

How are decisions made in different communities, and what role is played by individuals, political parties, pressure and community groups, religious organisations?

How do community decisions about, eg. transport, work, affect different individuals and groups within the community?

How do community decisions affect the physical environment and non-human world?

Concepts: community, interdependence, sustainability, rights, responsibility, scarcity, power

Question 8: In what ways can the welfare of individuals and societies be maintained?

What makes up our welfare?

What do individuals need for their well-being?

How do the decisions of other people, and of governments, affect our welfare?

What responsibilities do we have for our own welfare?

What rights and responsibilities should we have for our own welfare?

What kinds of responsibilities do local, national and international communities have for our welfare?

What differences of welfare exist between individuals and between groups?

What differences of welfare exist between nations?

Why do differences exist between people, groups and nations?

How should we respond to these differences?

Concepts: welfare, health, wealth, rights, responsibility, equality, inequality, freedom, scarcity, choice, justice

Question 9: On what basis do people make decisions when faced with particular choices?

What basic needs do we have as individuals? How do these differ from our wants?

Why do we have to make choices about our basic needs and wants? What influences the particular choices we make?

What sorts of choices do people have to make during the course of their lives?

How are their choices influenced by things such as culture, moral beliefs, religion, economic and social circumstances?

How do the choices people make affect others?

What choices do governments and non-government organisations have to make about how best to satisfy people's needs and wants?

What impact do the choices they make have on people and on the physical and non-human world?

Concepts: scarcity, choice, need, want, opportunity cost, division of labour, sustainability, rights, responsibility

Question 10: What is our relationship to the non-human world?

What different beliefs and attitudes do people have towards the non-human world?

How and why have these beliefs and attitudes varied?

How are our attitudes and beliefs about the non-human world influenced by religion, moral codes, culture, political and economic arrangements?

What impact can human decisions and actions have upon the non-human world?

What responsibility do we have towards the non-human world?

What responsibility do governments and non-government organisations have towards the non-human world?

Concepts: sustainability, interdependence, culture, belief, morality, rights, responsibility

Question 11: In what ways have people sought to explain the universe and to give meaning to their lives?

What different explanations do people have for the universe?

How and why have some of these explanations varied?

How and why do explanations sometimes vary across different cultures?

In what ways do we search to give meaning and purpose to our lives?

What contributions do religion, philosophy, science, political beliefs, make to our search for purpose and meaning?

Concepts: Morality, power, culture, belief

This is our framework. We hope that it is a useful 'high level planning tool' for primary and secondary teachers, and helps them to plan for the personal development of their pupils within and across the areas of the taught curriculum. It is designed to enable them to do this in ways which span the cross-curricular themes; ensure an equal opportunities perspective; and address the different aspects of personal development as outlined by OFSTED. We believe that the framework is most effective if it is part of a whole institutional approach and thus explicitly linked to a school's core values and ethos and is embedded in policies and development plans. The framework can help to shape a school's values and reaffirm their existence across the school. We are conscious that the framework does not provide an easy solution for ensuring provision for personal development; it is not a 'quick fix' model. Rather, it requires teachers to reflect on their practice and poses major challenges to many of the assumptions and ways of working within our schools.

This chapter has reviewed some of the important initiatives for pupils' personal development which have taken place over the past few years. We have also offered the reader a revised framework for planning and implementing provision for personal development in primary and secondary schools. The framework is offered as part of a continuing debate about personal development in whole school curriculum planning. That debate must be initiated and sustained by teachers working from 'below' but also by those in positions of authority and influence within the educational system.

References

Buck, M. and Inman, S. (1992) *Curriculum Guidance No 1: Whole School Provision for Personal and Social Development: the Role of the Cross Curricular Elements.* Centre for Cross Curricular Initiatives Goldsmiths College

Buck, M. and Inman, S. (1993) *Curriculum Guidance No 2: Re-affirming Values: Practical Case Studies in Implementing Cross Curricular Dimensions, Themes and Skills.* Centre for Cross Curricular Initiatives Goldsmiths College

Burke, H. (1993) 'PSHE and the Cross Curricular Elements' in Buck, M. and Inman, S. *op.cit.*

Caring for the Earth (1991) IUCN/UNEP/WWF Earthscan

Dearing, R. (1993) *The National Curriculum and its Assessment.* SCAA

Department of Education and Science (1989) *Curriculum Matters 14: Personal and Social Education from 5-16.* HMSO

National Commission on Education (1993) *Learning to Succeed.* Heinemann

National Curriculum Council (1993) *Spiritual and Moral Development; a discussion paper.* NCC

Office for Standards in Education (1994) *Spiritual, Moral, Social and Cultural Development.* OFSTED

Richardson, R. (1992) Identities and Justice: themes and concerns in education for citizenship. *Journal of Moral Education* Vol 21 No 3

Scott, D. (1993) 'Promoting values through Geogrpahy' in Buck, M. and Inman, S. (eds) *op. cit.*

Scottish Consultative Council on the Curriculum (1991) *Values in Education.*

Scottish Office Education Department (1993) *Personal and Social Development 5-14*

Selby, D. (1995) *EarthKind.* Trentham Books and EarthKind.

Chapter 2

Equal opportunities and personal development

Helena Burke

> The school has a clear policy which it monitors. Teachers appreciate how factors such as ethnicity, bilingualism, gender, social circumstances and giftedness may affect learning; they know how to plan work and organise and manage classes to take account of different needs of pupils whilst maintaining consistently high expectations.
> (*OFSTED: Guidance on the Inspection Schedule, Equality of Opportunity*, OFSTED, 1993 p.56)

The massive changes in education since 1988 have meant that equal opportunities have moved a long way down the agenda of educational issues. We as teachers have recently had to concern ourselves with National Curriculum, SATs, LMS, changes to the National Curriculum, changes to SATs etc. Classroom teachers committed to equal opportunities for our pupils have found it a constant struggle to keep it alive as an issue in our classrooms, with little or no opportunity to keep it to the forefront at a whole school level, or to share good practice or develop it within new learning contexts. That is not to say that there have not been some exciting developments but I am surely not alone in often failing in recent years to reflect upon just how effectively I am working toward equal opportunities in my classroom (and more recently with my students in Teacher Education).

In both settings I have been fortunate enough to work in institutions which have a commitment to equal opportunities. This is not universally the case and I would be interested to know how many schools which did not previously have an equal opportunities policy have felt any concern that this should be a priority or should be part of their school development plan. Or indeed how many schools have followed the response of one school noted by Debbie Epstein (1994), which denied that they needed to be less prominent on equal opportunities in order to retain or improve their market position now that there was open enrolment.

In this chapter I reiterate the importance of equal opportunities for the personal and social development of our pupils and argue that the present post-Dearing moratorium on change in education may well be the time for us to begin again to share good practice and develop equal opportunities within the National Curriculum and OFSTED frameworks. I consider some of the ways in which we can build on our achievements to develop equal opportunities work in the future, drawing examples from the humanities subjects which I have taught for a number of years in inner city schools.

Why equal opportunities?

I would begin by examining what I mean by equal opportunities in the context of pupils' Personal and Social Development.

Buck and Inman (1992) suggest that one aim of Personal and Social Development is to help pupils become:

> adults who are at ease with themselves on a personal and interpersonal level, who can make informed judgements about the world and who have the knowledge and the tools either to sustain or change that world (Buck and Inman, 1992 p.7).

I believe an awareness of issues of equality is an integral part of PSD, by developing pupils' understanding of the ways in which they are subject to the social constructions of others. As part of recreating such social constructions, pupils can begin to make sense of their experiences, educational and otherwise. The Personal and Social Development of the young people in our schools plays a part in creating our future society.

Numerous ministers for education have acknowledged this, most recently in the clear links drawn between RE teaching (of Christian values!), moral education, and the creation of a society free of crime. Although many would reject such a simplistic cause and effect model, I believe we must acknowledge our role in shaping our future society. We cannot pretend to offer a 'value free' education in our schools. Pupils are developing attitudes around 'race', gender, gay and lesbian sexuality and a whole range of other issues, whether or not we choose to acknowledge this explicitly. They learn values and attitudes in our classrooms, whether or not we remember that we are teaching them alongside the National Curriculum. We need explicitly to discuss and decide what those values and attitudes should be if we are to ask, what kind of society do we want? It is through understanding their own experiences that pupils can develop a capacity to challenge and change and to develop a future society in which cultures can develop and learn from each other.

I believe that to explore such ideas as part of their personal development also plays a central role in pupils' academic achievement and in the opportunities they have to realise their intellectual potential. By no means is there agreement that an awareness of issues of oppression, conflict and equality is an important part of this development. I would argue that if our schools are to become institutions striving for equality of opportunity then we need look at the links between achievement and an awareness of issues of equality and inequality. I believe there must be space for pupils to explore a range of values and attitudes in order to recognise both the obstacles they face and their own responsibility to strive against prejudices and attitudes which may hamper the achievement of others. If pupils have opportunities to explore their own experiences in the light of others' and if they have opportunities to establish their own identity and self-worth, we can provide them with the means to take a critical approach to the school curriculum and attain greater control over their own achievement. We need to provide opportunities for the pupils to become personally engaged in the curriculum. It is not enough for them to learn 'about' issues of equality; they must be able to explore what they mean for their own lives.

A brief history

It is important to determine how great the impact of the ERA was upon equal opportunities work in schools, by asking how much had been achieved previously. The period of greatest development of explicit teaching about equal opportunities appears to have been during the hey-day of the Metropolitan Councils and Education Authorities in the 1980s. For myself this meant working for the Inner London Education Authority which was one of the number of LEAs promoting the development of equal opportunities work in schools. This developed through the work of the range of groups playing a role in local government in the 1970s, in many cases groups who had not traditionally had a voice, such as the GLC Women's Committee. Changes had also been occurring on the national stage, with legislation such as the Race Relations Act (1976) and the Sex Discrimination Act (1975). Clearly the legislation was prompted by the work of numerous pressure groups, among them the black community organising around education, for example in establishing Saturday schools. However, there was also action of a different kind from groups such as the National Front, which forced the hand of the government.

In the early '80s, London and other LEAs began to develop recommendations to schools. In 1981 the ILEA set up a monitoring programme of the levels of achievement of those pupils from:

> different social classes, from different ethnic backgrounds and from both sexes. (ILEA, *Race, Sex and Class 2. Multi-Ethnic Education in Schools*, 1983 p.6)

As a part of this, schools were asked to re-evaluate their curriculum and organisation. This was a very different situation from the post-1988 educational era. It was a period when schools in certain areas were being instructed by their LEAs to show how they intended to raise the profile of equal opportunities for pupils from all cultural and 'racial' backgrounds. Indeed the ILEA identified for us the priorities which schools should be dealing with and included among them was clear reference to the idea of raising awareness of issues of racism as part of a young person's personal and social development.

> The analysis of developments in the field of race ... leads to the conclusion that priority needs to be given to four related issues: *the*

creation of a programme of anti-racist teaching; the establishment of proper forms of representation on the Authority of black people; the development of bilingual teaching; and the organisation of strategies to overcome underachievement by black pupils (my italics) (ILEA, *Race, Sex and Class 2. Multi-Ethnic Education in Schools*, 1983 p.16)

Work on gender and sexuality followed. Although this might now appear to have been a 'golden age' for equal opportunities in schools, this was not the true experience of working under the ILEA and like-minded education authorities at the time. There were always questions about how commitments on paper translated into reality and there was always dispute over degrees of action, most clearly expressed in the distinctions drawn between the multicultural approach and the more up-front antiracist stance some of us urged. However, whilst there may never have been a utopian period, the first part of the 1980s was definitely a very exciting time to be working in one of the more progressive LEAs. Equality was seen as central to education and ways of raising issues of equality within our classrooms were being developed.

In the later half of the 80s the climate began to change quite drastically. Clearly education does not operate in a vacuum and the advancing attack of the New Right on local government and education authorities, championed by particular sections of the popular press, began to make its impact. And so we saw the infamous scares about 'looney left' schools, exemplified by the allegation that 'Baa Baa Black Sheep' had been banned in one school. One political party advertisement for the 1987 general election, attacked the London Borough of Haringey's work in the field of raising awareness of equal opportunities issues in particular:

My name is Betty Sheridan. I live in Hackney. I'm married with 2 children. *And I'm scared.*
If you vote LABOUR they'll go on teaching my kids about GAYS AND LESBIANS instead of giving them proper lessons. (quoted by D. Cooper, in Jones. C. and Mahony, P., 1989, p.52)

Some ILEA staff would argue that the inspectorate's document, *The Teaching Of Controversial Issues in Schools* (1986) helped construct a discourse which divided education between 'safe' and controversial issues (whatever the intention of those working on the document), thus emphasising which issues would be exploited by the New Right. The legislation which followed, including Section 28 of the Local Government Act (1988) and the Education Reform Act (1988), had massive implications for equal opportunities.

The greatest effect of Section 28 was the change in agenda. Exploration of lesbian and gay life-styles was now believed by many to be contrary to the act. Six years later I am still being asked by my students in teacher education whether they are allowed to discuss such issues in the classroom.

The Education Reform Act (ERA) 1988

The full impact of the ERA for equal opportunities is too extensive to encompass here. However, one vital aim was to diminish the power of local authorities. They became a much weaker link in the chain of education and are no longer powerful promoters of initiatives in schools. The impact in terms of the personal and social development of pupils is immense. Whole departments and subjects were lost in schools that raced to follow what appeared to be required by the National Curriculum. It must be more than happy coincidence for the Conservatives that such subjects as Social Studies, ideal forums for discussion of issues of equal opportunities, did not form part of the statutory orders, while the orders for subjects which did form part of the curriculum lost many of the aspects of their work which explored equal opportunities. Geography was so heavily content-based that it became incredibly difficult to pursue enquiry about the world as presented to us. The public debate about what constituted school history stressed the necessity for pupils to learn 'facts' (largely about Britain). A case was made for excluding questioning or relating historical events to the present day. However, the end result did allow a greater capacity for pupils' personal and social development than did the geography curriculum. Kate Moorse (1994) draws our attention to the fact that:

> the statutory order conceives both educational and historical aims as integrated one with the other and not the former as adjunct to the latter.

and that:

> stronger statements were made and more items given the force of law in the history statutory order than most, if not all other subjects, e.g.

36

experiences of men and women, cultural diversity of societies studied, IT and the requirement that the history curriculum addresses the cross curricular themes. (Buck, M., Inman, S. and Moorse, K., 1994 p.6).

The PESC formula supported the requirement that history should be studied from a range of perspectives. We were also given the Cross-Curricular Themes and Dimensions. Their usefulness in keeping some of the issues of personal and social development on the agenda should not be underestimated.

Many teachers and schools used the Themes and Dimensions as ways of ensuring that work developed on equality issues was not lost. Statements such as:

> schools need to foster a climate in which equality of opportunity is supported by a policy to which the whole school subscribes and in which positive attitudes to gender equality, cultural diversity and special needs of all kinds are actively promoted (NCC, 1990, p.3)

potentially favoured the continued development of work in equal opportunities, looking at the promotion of attitudes and values in addition to or as part of access to the curriculum. However, these documents were of uncertain status, not statutory but advisory. At a time when departments were desperately struggling to understand and deliver the statutory orders, any teacher with responsibility for the Themes and Dimensions could tell you how difficult it was to persuade staff to take them seriously. The NCC also failed to provide us with a realistic model for curriculum development. The themes and dimensions were described as 'cross curricular' but no thought appeared to have been given to how such an approach could be applied in the context of subject documents that were produced in isolation from each other, so recreating the fragmentation that good practitioners had worked against for many years.

The present day context

Where does this leave us now? Whilst some LEAs may still be keen to promote initiatives in equal opportunities, their power to enforce has been severely diminished, and whilst there was space within the original statutory orders for committed teachers to continue with such work, it was clear that the spirit of them was not in tune with such concerns.

I suggest that there are currently three forces involved in developing work in equal opportunities. The first lies within the elements of the more recent legislation, the *Dearing Review of the National Curriculum* and the OFSTED inspection framework. Secondly, I believe that notions of 'quality' education as originally presented by the New Right are beginning to be deconstructed by more progressive educationalists in a way that shows 'quality' to be unachievable without equality (Runnymede Trust, 1993).

Finally, I believe that the evidence of recent projects in schools shows us that the lessons of the past still hold true. A major force in ensuring that equality issues are raised in our schools will come from classroom practice of individuals and groups of teachers. Let us look at each of these forces more closely.

i. The Dearing Review and OFSTED Framework

Does Dearing (1994) really provide us with an environment in which we can again begin to develop pupils' personal and social skills in the area of equal opportunities? Dearing presents us with what is in many ways a reductionist model. The cross- curricular themes do not seem to be retained within the governments' guidelines, so it will be left to individual schools to decide which elements will be kept, in order to provide for pupils' personal and social development. However, in the revised guidelines *do* allow the *possibility* of exploring issues of equality, created by the reduction in prescribed content. To take examples from the Humanities, the guidelines for history facilitate greater study of 20th century history and thus exploration of issues which, having more immediate relevance to pupils' lives, can play a part in raising awareness of equal opportunities. The reduction of content and revised approach to geography encourages the idea that:

> Pupils should be required to develop their skills, knowledge and understanding through geographical enquiries across the whole range of scales, using field work where appropriate. Enquiry questions should be largely of the 'What/where is it?', 'What is it like?', 'How did it get like this?', 'How and why has it changed?', 'How might it change?' type (SCAA May, 1994, p.12).

This again allows a planning approach which is *questioning* about the world as it is presented to us. For me this is central to incorporating issues of equal opportunities in our classes, and thus in acknowledging our role in the personal development of pupils, whatever the subject.

OFSTED, on the other hand, provides explicit requirements to bring equal opportunities back onto the agenda of our school development plans.

The Framework and the changes made within it should be viewed critically, but we should not underestimate the importance of sections 5 and 7. The political context may well have changed radically from that of 1983 when authorities instructed schools to move to a programme of 'anti-racist teaching', yet we are once again being told that we have a specific responsibility for equal opportunity as part of pupils' personal and social development. The learning outcomes suggested by OFSTED for spiritual, moral, social and cultural development would support this belief. Inspectors are to observe whether:

> ...pupils give evidence of moral development if, at a level appropriate to their age and ability, they display:...
>
> *personal values* in relation to ...
> local, national and world issues
> With reference to such issues as:
>
> the individual and the community — rights, duties and responsibilities; war and peace; human rights; exploitation and aid; medical ethics; environmental issues; equal opportunities (sex, race, disability, class) (OFSTED, 1994, p.13- 14).

This is further supported by the framework for inspection itself. The opening quotation of this chapter shows exactly what we should be doing in our schools in order to ensure equality of opportunity. Within this we are being asked to: 'take account of the different needs of pupils " to work toward a situation where: all may achieve good standards and develop their talents to the full (OFSTED, 1993, p.56).

The link between the development of values and attitudes relating to equality, and pupils developing their talents to the full explored earlier in this chapter, is I believe, also acknowledged by OFSTED in that they are concerned to see: 'how well the policy is *understood*, implemented and monitored' (my italics) (OFSTED, 1994 p.29) and one of the ways in which inspectors will evaluate this is through: 'observation in the classroom and other school contexts: and discussion with pupils and staff' (p.57). Thus the inspection procedure demands that we can demonstrate that our pupils have an understanding of issues relating to equal opportunities.

ii. Quality and Equality

In terms of whole school focus or 'climate', a number of recent works have helped us to bring issues of equal opportunities back onto school agendas through quality assurance. Kathryn Riley (1994) draws our attention to the similarities in the views exemplified by some LEAs in the early 1980s and now in the 90s, in terms of 'equality' and 'quality'. As long as we remain aware of the ideological differences in the origin of these terms, I believe we can usefully parallel them in our attempts to return equal opportunities to the arena of whole school development. If we see the pre-ERA context as one in which many were working with notions of equality as central to their practice, then we can trace this thread back to the 1944 Education act and its aims of egalitarianism. What we see embodied in the 1988 Act is the New Right view that:

> The pursuit of egalitarianism is over. (Kenneth Baker, Secretary of State for Education, quoted in Riddell and Brown, 1992).

The origin of this view can be traced to the Black Papers of the 1970s. Riley (1994) illustrates how the dominant discourse established 'quality' as something which had been sacrificed at the expense of 'equality' and how this discourse prepared the ground for the ERA:

> The charge put forward by central government was that schools — and in particular comprehensive schools — had failed because they had pursued egalitarian goals at the expense of efficiency and effectiveness. Local authorities were accused by central government of not having made the pursuit of quality a major objective.

So quality was to be introduced through the market place and to be measured by SATs, league tables and open enrolment.

However, seven years on, educationalists are re-examining the terms, showing that far from being mutually exclusive, quality cannot be achieved without equality. As Riley suggests, we need to ask the question: 'quality for whom?"

Frith and Mahony extend this further:

> ...what many have failed to realise is that quality and equality are inextricably linked. How can we attempt to raise standards through the delivery of a new curriculum and with new modes of assessment, without using the knowledge we have gained about the differential effect of teaching style and grouping on pupil performance? How can we hope to improve our assessment techniques if we ignore what we have learnt about differences in motivation and performance between girls and boys? (Frith, R. and Mahony, P., 1994, p.1).

The links also hold true for raising awareness of equal opportunities issues as part of personal and social development. How can we hope to educate the whole child, to provide for the spiritual, moral, social and cultural development of our pupils, without taking account of decades of good practice in whole school equal opportunities policies and practices? Indeed, the policy of one school, written before the term 'quality in education' had been adopted as a way of justifying league tables and the like, recognised this:

> The central aim of the school is to provide the best educational experiences for all its pupils. This can only be achieved through the delivery of a *high quality education* catering for the needs of all students.... (my italics).

Can schools really claim to be providing quality education if they are denying some pupils access to the curriculum, if they are failing to help some pupils in developing a positive self- identity, if they are failing to enhance pupils' understanding of their own and each others' culture? In short if they are denying some pupils the opportunity to realise their potential and their power to take their part in the creation of our future society?

iii. Classroom Practice

Having established that the national inspection framework supports equality issues and that the concern of all schools to provide quality education *must* take account of equality, let us consider the role of the individual teacher.

41

Frith and Mahony's work (1994) shows us that developing *your own* classroom practice with colleagues, on issues which we regard as of real educational importance, that engages teachers anew and provides an essential force in effecting whole school development:

> by including gender within the topic based curriculum, and supporting gender based work with improved resourcing and guidance *linked to the curriculum*, and to the promotion of appropriate teaching methods, I would hope that the marginalisation of gender issues would be avoided. There will be a shift in emphasis for gender ... towards what they should be learning in class as part of the overt curriculum. (Smith, M. in Mahony, P. and Frith, R., 1994, p.101)

The reality of this is illustrated through the Gender Action Project which the book charts. The Runnymede Trust (1993) publication discussed below similarly unites quality and equality, in relation to race.

Planning for Equal Opportunities

Addressing equal opportunities within the taught curriculum relates to teaching and planning styles which have been identified as good practice for some time. It is important that work in the area of equal opportunities enters into the pupils' way of seeing and understanding the world, rather than just being something which pupils learn *about*. So key questions must be linked to learning outcomes and this has implications for styles of teaching and learning. Pupils need to be given opportunities to consider questions of equality in relation to their own lives and also to engage in activities which provide opportunities to try out different ways of organising their relationships with others. Teaching about issues of equality and inequality in relation only to a specific historical setting, other people or a distant geographical location, does not allow an understanding of equal opportunities to become part of pupils' *personal* development. This personal understanding is essential to help pupils to develop a more global commitment. If we do not make the links clearly between these 'other' settings and their own lives or give them the opportunity to engage in different ways of organising their relationships through active learning tasks, we deny pupils opportunities to become: 'adults who have the capacity to promote justice and equality, who are critical thinkers, and are informed about the world' (Buck, M., Inman, S. and Moorse K., 1994, p.11).

The Runnymede Trust (1993) indicators of good practice in providing what they call 'Equality Assurance' (Fig.1) can serve as checklists when planning work which examines equality issues as they relate to pupils' interpretation of the world.

In the example overleaf I have tried to use the Geography indicators (all basic curriculum subjects are tackled this way in the book) to check the kinds of key questions and concepts which are central to the scheme of work. Linking all these to specific learning outcomes helps pupils not only to increase their knowledge of such issues but also to develop personally and socially. The learning outcomes devised by Buck and Inman (see chapter 1) *demand* such an approach. For example, pupils should be: 'able to take responsibility for own actions and the effects of these actions upon others'.

This is clearly more than a matter of pupils *knowing* that their actions have implications for others — it guides future behaviour.

The examples in Fig 1 involve only aspects of the geography curriculum and Fig. 2 attempts to show how ideas of making equality issues part of pupils' personal and social development brings together different elements of good practice.

These examples show the opportunities for issues of equal opportunity to be raised within the Geography draft guidelines for key stage 3. They are not intended to cover all aspects of the planning for whole topics, but rather to draw out specific elements which would fit within an overall plan.

In themselves the questions and concepts will not guarantee a particular set of learning outcomes, but they do show an approach to planning which the lessening of content in the statutory orders will allow and which facilitates meeting the OFSTED criteria. The styles of teaching and learning adopted and the ways in which pupils can be encouraged to see these issues as having relevance to their own lives, will determine the effectiveness of learning outcomes relating to personal and social development.

Fig 1: from Runnymede Trust: *Equality Assurance in schools; quality, identity, society.* Trentham Books, 1993 (p.32).

GEOGRAPHY
Indicators of good practice

1 Pupils draw on their experience of family and community in relation to social trends, processes and changes, and reflect on their own personal experience and sense of space.

2 Pupils recognise differences and commonalities in humankind's relationships with the physical environment, and in measures to improve the quality of life through trade and economic development.

3 Pupils recognise that all economic development takes place within a global context, and that local decisions and processes in any one locality affect, and are affected by, decisions and processes in other localities. In studies of development, pollution, stewardship and conservation they appreciate the global and international dimensions of the issues.

4 In studies of economic development in Europe and developing countries, pupils are aware of differences in power and influence, benefits, gains and disadvantages, and of a range of theoretical perspectives.

5 Negative images of developing countries in the media, for example images which portray developing countries as poverty-stricken and 'backward', depending passively on aid from richer countries, are challenged and corrected.

6 The study of decision-making and planning processes in relation to alternative land uses, develops pupils' understanding of moral and political concepts such as conflict of interest, justice and fairness, rights and obligations, responsibility, and democracy.

7 Pupils recognise that migration, population movement and settlement are recurring experiences in human history, and they study both commonalities and variations in migrants' and settlers' experiences.

8 Pupils use a variety of source material when studying other countries.

9 Links are made with other subjects and with National Curriculum cross-curricular themes: economic and industrial understanding, environmental education and health education.

Figure 2: Geography Key Stage 3 Brazil

Focus of Study	Key Questions	Key Concepts
The characteristics of Rainforest and the Impact of Human Activity	What is the importance of the rain forest to the human and non-human world? How has the human world worked with and against the resources of the rainforest?	Ecosystems Sustainability Exploitation Interdependence

Indicators of Good Practice — Runnymede Trust (1993)

2. Pupils recognise differences and commonalities in humankind's relationships with the physical environment, and in measures to improve the quality of life through trade and economic development.

6. The study of decision making and planning processes in relation to alternative land uses, develops pupil's understanding of moral and political concepts such as conflict of interest, justice and fairness, rights and obligations, responsibility and democracy.

Learning Outcomes — Buck and Inman (1993)

— able to maintain effective interpersonal relationships within a moral framework

— able to promote a concern for all forms of life, now and in the future

Suggested Activities

— Exploration of what the rainforest contributes to the lives of different characters both in the locality of the rainforest and globally

— Working teams taking the role of different interest groups involved in the rainforest e.g. indigenous peoples, developers, the government. Analysis of the benefits of different future plans for the rainforest which would they support? Which would bring benefits to most people?

— Link to a more local development project, exploring from range of perspectives.

Focus of Study	Key Questions	Key Concepts
How is the Country of Study Set Within a Global Context?	How do communities relate to each other?	Interdependence Exploitation Power

Indicators of Good Practice, Geography — Runnymede Trust (1993)

3. Pupils recognise that all economic development takes place within a global context, and that local decisions and processes in any one locality affect, and are affected by, decisions and processes in other localities. In studies of development, pollution, stewardship and conservation they appreciate the global and international dimensions of issues.

Learning Outcomes — Buck and Inman (1993)

— concerned about promoting fairness, justice and equality on an interpersonal, societal and global level

— skilled in how to work collaboratively and autonomously

Suggested Activities

— An analysis of interdependence within the school community

— A simulation of global trading relations (Christian Aid Trading Game) involving choices between co-operation and conflict

— A role-play debate exploring the benefits of or exploitation by multi-national companies in Brazil.

45

Conclusions

I believe we have reason in the mid-1990s to be optimistic about the future of pupils' personal and social development and the role in this of an awareness of equality issues. OFSTED's recognition of the importance of issues of equality, the growing understanding that equality must form part of quality education, and the continued commitment of teachers who have the space and the means to develop such work give reason for qualified optimism. We need to build upon the struggles and achievements of the 1970s and 80s and continue to investigate the opportunities within the National Curriculum and throughout the whole school for raising equality issues. And if we accept that pupils' personal and social development is part of our responsibility as educators then we must continue to ensure that they become aware of issues of equality.

References

Buck, M. and Inman, S. (eds.) (1991) *Curriculum Guidance No.1*. Goldsmiths' Centre for Cross Curricular Initiatives

Buck, M. and Inman, S. (eds.) (1993) *Curriculum Guidance No.2*. Goldsmiths' Centre for Cross Curricular Initiatives

Buck, M., Inman, S. and Moorse, K. (1994) *Educating The Whole Child: Cross-Curricular Themes Within The History Curriculum*. Historical Association

Cooper, D. in Jones, C. and Mahony, P. (eds.) (1989) *Learning Our Lines*. Women's Press

Epstein, D. (ed.) (1994) *Challenging Lesbian and Gay Inequalities in Education*. Open University Press

Frith, R. and Mahony, P. (eds.) (1994) *Promoting Quality and Equality in Schools*. David Fulton

Inner London Education Authority (1983) *Race, Sex and Class 2. Multi-Ethnic Education in Schools*. ILEA

National Curriculum Council (1993) *The Whole Curriculum*. NCC

OFSTED (1993) *Framework for Inspection*. HMSO

OFSTED (1994) *Spiritual, Moral, Social and Cultural Development, An OFSTED discussion paper*. HMSO

Riley, K. (1994) *Quality and Equality*. Cassell

Runnymede Trust (1993) *Equality Assurance in School*. Trentham Books

Schools Curriculum and Assessment Authority (1994) *Consultation on the National Curriculum*. SCAA

SCAA (1994) *Geography in the National Curriculum, Draft Proposals*. SCAA

SCAA (1994) *History in the National Curriculum, Draft Proposals*. SCAA

SCAA (1994) *National Curriculum Orders, Second page-proof copy*. SCAA

Chapter 3

Race and cultural diversity

Pauline Lyseight-jones

This chapter begins by describing some of the difficulties in engaging with a discussion of race and cultural identity in the context of citizenship. It then indicates some of the areas which remain important for the healthy development of the individual. Through a brief account of OFSTEDs indicators of school failure, some specific points are made about the more particular impact of race on these indicators.

An account of discussions with primary age students draws out three areas which they emphasise: name-calling, bullying and fairness and justice. This section ends with a call for the development of systems in schools which allow students the real opportunity to change things in school. It is followed by an account of discussions by secondary students, which focus on fairness, help from teachers and race issues. The chapter concludes with an account of a mentoring project which was set up in an urban comprehensive school.

To begin

School is isolating. It requires the individual to stand on their own. It requires sense to be made of a complex network of influences and people. This scenario allows people to get lost, to feel small, to feel defensive and alienated, In the best of schools, it allows the individual to grow, giving due respect and regard to themselves and others.

The discussion on race which now locates itself under citizenship also has some firm niches elsewhere — equal opportunities, development education and so on. These antecedents contribute to an analysis which accepts that race and heritage impact on the society in general and on individuals in particular.

The lessons of anti-racism, human rights education and other equity-based education '-isms' lay down increasingly recognised as a package of attributes or wishes which are of value to our children. How these attributes are interpreted depends on the philosophical stance and cultural base that is being employed.

The package

For people to grow, there needs to be

- recognition — I can be accepted here
- respect — I can be heard here
- self-esteem — I can feel good about me
- an outward eye — I can show insight into the circumstances of others
- influence — I can make things happen.

This package has the potential to lead to a healthy individual who can then develop desire and motivation to become the best and most successful person which they can be. Additionally, the school which supports students in their personal development has to display genuine need — it is difficult to belong if there is no place for you, there is nothing of value which you have which the organisation values and desires. The school has also to conscientiously offer choice. Reaching ones potential is hard if the choices are essentially between a rock and a hard place.

The discussion below accepts that the package of attributes are necessary for all students but that it may be even more essential to develop in people who are not part of the dominant culture. (Clearly, in many circumstances, girls would be the target group — and it is testimony to the emphasis, through equal opportunities, on girls self-esteem, achievement and access to choice that there is the all too familiar backlash which requires us to consider whether or not we have, in fact, let down our boys.)

Histories and views

The need for authentic voices has been chronicled elsewhere. The development of oral history work, the collection of memoirs of activities of black people in the Services in World War II, and the work many individuals in building up black archives, chronicling histories, has given rise to extensive argument and debate. Much of the work arose from reactions to the engagement in racist or discriminatory and prejudicial activities which seemed to institutionalise low self-esteem and low achievement leading to poor life chances amongst, firstly black students and adults of African-Caribbean origin. This circumstance was exacerbated by the residue of colonialism and the activity of the class structure.

But students who are black or Asian in Britain today cannot be said to be without history or significant culture. For black and Asian students in Britain today, such race-related work is itself both fact and history. New authentic voices need to be heard. This discussion can not, therefore, be advanced through the recollections, conclusions and analysis of solely first or even second generation settlers in Britain. Today's students have to talk.

Accordingly, this piece owes much to discussions with groups of young people, from a range of backgrounds representing those in primary and secondary phases of education. Together we tried to get a fix on what school is about and what education is about currently. If this means that the specific issue of race does not isolate itself in the way it had in the past, then so be it. It may be seen as a measure of past success in the area of equalities issues.

The school days of people such as myself could be seen as an odd mix of isolation and security; in my case, the oddness of a good and eager reader being given books to read from the infant school library of the ilk of *Little Black Sambo*. In secondary school the impact of class compounded the sense of other-worldliness, the selective system being in full flow. Suddenly, fathers were understood to wear suits to work and were managers or were in business. The curriculum was equally alien — requiring the parsing of sentences — the phrase, 'In apposition to anticipatory 'it' ' is forever riveted on my memory, as are the three major rivers of China. I can draw Artesian wells and I know more about the climbing activities of the dodder than is necessary to build a fully rounded personality. The priority of school was not for it to fit the student but for the student to fit — in much the same way as one is advised to throw strands of spaghetti against a kitchen wall to test whether they are cooked — if they stick they are, if they fall they're not.

Wonderful, wasted, unambitious times were had — and if the students were male and black, add to this: 'disruptive'.

The above reflection leads to a puzzle and a problem. What is the extent to which race and cultural identity presents as a specific issue requiring distinct attention?

A dawning

Following much debate, the area of spiritual, moral, social and cultural development of students has become part of the school inspection schedule. In the context of schools and education the Office for Standards in Education recognises that these areas are tangible enough to be detected, inspected and evaluated. The evaluation of cultural development expects that:

> it is to be judged by how well the school prepares pupils to understand aspects of their own and other cultural environments, be these relig-ious, social, aesthetic or ethnic, and by the pupils' response to this provision, which may be through literature, music, technology, art and design, dance, sport and other media (OFSTED 1994).

Such a definition clearly allows for multicultural and anti-racist work to begin and continue, to develop and to be taken into account when judging the quality of schools and the education which they provide. Such a definition allows for the study of morris dancing, too. For a teacher or a whole staff group this definition gives the freedom to describe a curriculum, through delivery and through content, which more overtly and explicitly responds to cultural diversity in Britain.

Within the context of the *Handbook for the Inspection of Schools* (OFSTED, 1994), there is guidance on the range of factors which must be taken into account when an inspection team considers that a school may be failing. Such factors fall into four categories — standards of achievements, quality of education provided, efficiency of the school and pupils' spiritual, moral, social and cultural development. To assist in discerning quality in these areas, a questions are posed within each of the categories. For the purpose of this discussion, the questions which seem to be more centrally concerned with race are indicated with additional comment [1].

Questions to be answered

- *Is there underachievement by the majority of pupils or consistently among particular groups of pupils?*

Underachievement may derive from a range of factors. In the context of this piece, the most relevant are students being given a poorly taught, badly planned and poorly matched curriculum with inadequate attention given to planning the most appropriate next steps for students, based on sound assessment practice.

The National Curriculum in either its old or new form, brings with it the entitlement for students to a broad based curriculum. The opening out of some areas, for example science, gives some students the change to explore new areas. This brings with it the possibility that the practical as well as the academic student may be motivated to learn. The greater emphasis on investigative modes of teaching and learning and the impact of cross-curricular work plus the growing importance of personal development education within the curriculum can only be seen as an advantage.

The analysis of student performance on a continuous basis needs development. Yet the growth of profiling, records of achievement and analysis of sub-group assessment results allows for planned emphasis on groups who were previously left to drift and fail. Historically, black and ethnic minority students have been seen to be part of this failing group. An attempt to counter underachievement amongst black students through the development of a mentoring programme is described later in this chapter; we move on now to the next question.

- *Do pupils make unsatisfactory progress in acquisition of knowledge, understanding and skills, and do they lack motivation?*

Motivation requires students to feel excitement and interest in the matter being dealt with. It requires a belief that the learning process itself will be worthwhile. It requires the student to feel that teaching and learning are taking place in an atmosphere of respect and acceptance. Overly didactic teaching featuring closed questions and a 'read my mind' form of enquiry on the part of the teacher have no place in the fostering of the motivated student. Teaching through telepathy tends to take little note of students' prior knowledge and experience. It does not encourage talk, nor the development of ideas or hypotheses, the realisation of multiple solutions or the growth of effective self-criticism and review. Where the culture of the school staff differs markedly from that of the students and where this difference is not taken into account when preparing for teaching, the potential of students to achieve and to be motivated to continue to achieve, remain hidden behind a fog of bewilderment.

- *Are the teachers' expectations of pupils' achievements low?*

Research like the purple arm-band experiment or the work which informed teachers that they had been given a group of high attainers when they had in fact been given the lowest attainers, show the effect of teacher expectation on student progress and the effect of adverse personal contacts on the self-esteem and mental health of students.

The purple arm-band experiment was replicated by using modified so that the variable was the colours of student's eyes[2]. Students with blue eyes were treated — on the first day — in a particularly affirming way. These American 9 year olds were not told why. Neither were their classmates. All began to understand that different treatments were being meted out and then the expected human response came. The favoured students grew, they blossomed. They also came to accept an accident of fate as a rationally acceptable reason for superiority. They began to see other less favoured classmates as deserving poorer treatment and of having less intrinsic value as people. The unfortunates with the wrong coloured eyes became withdrawn or angry, upset or disruptive. They had to fight to keep their self-worth and they, too, began to feel that they really were inferior to the other groups. When their teacher reversed the roles, claiming that it was people with brown eyes who were 'better', the children again conformed to expectations.[3]

Years after the experiment the students, now adults, were brought together again. Their memories of that time were both vivid and bitter.

In the second piece of research,[4] the students who were labelled as the high achieving group, even though previous assessment showed them not to be intellectually precocious, made significant leaps in their learning, their teacher praised them fulsomely, expected high achievement and helped students to solve the set problems and to complete the set tasks because she knew that they had it in them. She felt happy in her work because she was given the brightest group. She felt validated and proud.

It is not difficult to take messages from these two examples and locate them in the day-to-day operation of school and the treatment which is given to particular groups of students, sometimes girls, sometimes black and ethnic minority students.

The teacher who treats their teaching groups as stars will have as many stars as they wish, and the teacher who believe that they are working on the front line because they are in a multi- racial inner city school will have as many battles as they could wish for.

Low teacher expectation may arise through a teacher's insufficient understanding of the prior learning and knowledge which students bring to school and to the classroom. It may also arise through the operation of prejudicial attitudes. Confering with their students may help teachers with regard to prior knowledge, but attitude problems can be dealt with through the operation of structures in school which diminish the effect of any prejudicial attitudes — this would include analysis of assessment results, criterion-based student groupings as teaching or class groups, and structured inservice training programmes which encourage exploration of values and sustained work towards the development of the school as a healthy organisation[5].

Within the discussion of low expectation comes the all too frequent lack of understanding by teachers of the distinctions between students for whom English is an additional language and students who have special educational needs.[6] A report (OFSTED 1994) commenting on in-class support for minority ethnic communities states that:

> The most effective lessons included the use of specially prepared materials to match the pupils' levels of English and educational

experience, and tasks which enabled them to work purposefully with their peers and encouraged them to become increasingly independent of support... Section 11 teachers often used their knowledge of the pupils' culture and background to make the lesson more relevant to the minority ethnic pupils and to enrich the lesson for all. The best practice made a significant contribution to the confidence of the pupils, who were able to take a full part in the day to day activity of the school.[7]

- *Is there poor provision for [spiritual, moral, social and cultural] aspects of pupils' development?*

The discussion on aims to practice is becoming more relevant and vital. The expectation is that schools be actively concerned with an able to show that school aims are more than just platitudes. Many schools have school aims or mission statements which refer to the development of the whole student, the nurturing of independence, respect for oneself and others as well as a healthy appreciation of the world at large and its citizens. Quality statements follow, saying that high academic achievement is expected, with each student doing the best that they possibly can. In practice, the work of many schools locates primarily within the academic domain with the systematic and practical realisation of the spiritual, moral, social and cultural areas, the ethos and the hidden or the implicit curriculum package being less well developed [I admit it — I have difficulty with saris being on display and international evenings.] The obverse of this coin may be equally harmful — where the social needs of students perceived to come from disadvantaged backgrounds are the major business of the school, to the detriment of their academic and intellectual development. Primary schools have increasingly promoted work in these areas through the use of circle time[8] and other devices which allow students to offer to each other in controlled settings their experiences and their fears, their solutions to conflict and their perception of problems. Misconceptions may be dealt with and the group develops its own society and manages its own socialisation.

In the secondary sector, well-structured and sensitively managed tutorial work may perform the same function.

- *Are relationships with pupils poor — are they abrasive and confrontational?*

We used to be allowed to hit students in school. We can't any more. We have survived. Why do some teachers still bawl out students and use irony and sarcasm as weapons? Still less, why do some teachers feel able to write this offensiveness in students' work-books and convey such messages to other teachers and to the parents? There is no need.

Where relationships with students are generally poor, there are likely to be prevailing poor relationships amongst staff or a poor management team which allows such a circumstance of disrespect to continue and, possibly, flourish. This is an area which is most likely to bring parents school with murder (or at least wounding) in their hearts. The whole story is not necessarily told and the student is blamed for flying off the handle[9].

Confrontational and abrasive relationships, in the context of school can come from a misreading of verbal and non-verbal signals, different interpretations of authority and status, fundamental disrespect for the other party, lack of understanding of relevant social conventions and sometimes, fear born of prejudice.

Dealing with this is hard but the making of codes of conduct and the implementation of systems which minimise the need for confrontation are part of the solution. In writing this I have in mind disenfranchised, disenchanted black boys well into puberty, who are treated as people outside school and who have some status in their social group being shouted down or punished because of the colour of their shoes or somesuch silliness. I have written about this before, but I think it bears retelling. A fifteen year old black boy who had had his hair cut with two lines shaved into it, was put into internal exclusion in school, and was not allowed to work with the rest of his year group. His GCSE's were a disaster. He is a part-time window cleaner now. I know what he thought of his school and of the anguish which this contretemps caused his parents (his mother was the one who took him to get his hair cut) but the horror is what the school must think of him and countless students like him, what value they place on him. The awfulness of the message is nearly too sad to consider.

- *Are pupils regularly disruptive?*

This is a charge which is all to frequently levelled against black, or increasingly, Asian students. Or, more specifically, black and Asian boys. Discussions over the years with young black students features boring lessons, lack of respect (teacher to student and vice versa) and victimisation as motives or movers behind disruption in the classroom. What is often left unsaid is the extent to which the student is unclear of the task set and has no way to ask about it without being seen as unintelligent or troublesome.

This Catch-22 situation can also be observed in hospital wards. Post-operative patients complaining of pain may be told that they are exaggerating and those who stay silent but in pain are seen as good patients. Neither patient is getting what they need. In school, the Catch-22 scenario leads to increased bewilderment and more reason on the part of the student to use attack as the first form of defence.

- *Is the level of exclusion high?*

The Runnymede Trust has analysed the first fifty secondary school inspection reports where the inspections were carried out using the Framework for the Inspection of Schools.[10]

Among other explorations into the impact of equal opportunity factors within inspection the report looks at the incidence of exclusion and which groups of students were being excluded. Some schools show a disproportionate amount of ethnic minority students being excluded from secondary schools. Of these students the great majority are boys.

Exclusion tends to be linked with disaffection. We have explored aspects of disaffection above. That said, the report cites some schools where no exclusion occurred and where the socio-economic and ethnic composition of the school populations were similar to those which seemed to show excessive zeal. Luck cannot be the discriminating factor between the two circumstances. Exclusion takes away access to education.

- *Is there evidence of high levels of racial tension or harassment?*

This is one of the most pleasing aspects of the *Framework* — the explicit understanding that racism is not acceptable in schools, is counter-productive and is a contributory factor to the school as a failing institution.

Over the years, commentators have mapped out the damaging effects of racism on the society as a whole and on those on whom it is exercised in particular. The defining of racist activity through the simple axiom, racism equals prejudice plus power, offers an explanation to the mass but not the particular. It encourages a view of communities as essentially homogeneous. Increasingly, teaching staff are required to appreciate that there may be a race agenda in any kind of school, that that agenda will be linked with bullying, name-calling and with other aspects of school life which fall into pastoral, behavioural and disciplinary areas. Much has been published on these subjects. Activity to counter bullying and name-calling and to improve pastoral systems should also diminish the operation of racism.

Discussion with students

Primary age students

These students tended to focus on name-calling, bullying and fairness and justice.

Name-calling — there remains opportunity and inclination for students to insult each other through racist name-calling. This is not a simple matter of white against black. Some of the most vociferous and indignant students were Irish. They understood that racism operated against them. The effects of the troubles in Ireland cannot be minimised for these students. Nor can the effects of the range of centuries-old stereotypes and prejudices against the Irish as a group. International students whose ethnic origins were being mistaken felt both wrongly labelled and actively insulted.

Bullying — this has been an area of intense educational activity in primary schools. Just as the campaigns about 'Stranger Danger' and 'Just Say 'No'' gave rise to a new active vocabulary and a heightened awareness amongst young children so too has work on bullying increased the likelihood that students have the relevant vocabulary, are able to recognise bullying and know that it is not acceptable.[11]

Students are loath to admit to being bullies but some did admit to being bullied. Bullying seems to cross gender and ethnic boundaries. There seems to be no greater likelihood of the bully or the bullied being from an ethnic minority group. Bullies tend to be physically overpowering —

either actually or through implied threat. They tend not to operate on their own — bullies seem to need an audience, a posse or a crony. Most bullying takes place in playtime and lunchtimes and on the way home from school and teachers generally tended not to be present when bullying occurs, so they are not the authority figures at the times of the highest incidence of bullying.

Fairness and justice — students were clear about the school structures for making complaints but often felt that their complaints were being responded to inadequately. This was interwoven with issues which surrounded racist incidents and which expressed the internalisation of racist stereotypes. Examples were given of black students being told off for poor behaviour while other (non-black) students were not reprimanded. Additionally, students from all ethnic groups affirmed a picture of the word of the black student not being accepted until a white child affirmed that the circumstance or the proposition was correct. Students were also clear about which teachers favoured which children or groups. They gave examples of teaching staff being insensitive or using language to students which betrayed racist stereotyping or adverse bias.

For these primary age students the main arena for injustice is the playground. The role of the lunchtime supervisors seems to be crucial to ensure that the emphases within classrooms on the prohibition of racist name-calling and such like are seen as equally important outside of the given, teacher-delivered, classroom-located curriculum context. The supervisor's role in contributing to the hidden or implicit curriculum has been recognised by the growth of training courses for such supervisory staff on matters such as conflict resolution and behaviour management, as well as more positive and active sessions on organising playground games. Even so, students recognise that the way of dealing with conflict in playtime conflagrations is often to apportion no specific blame and to either punish all ('o.k. — all of you, stand by that wall until the end of play') or else tell complainer to keep away from their tormentor. What is clear to these students is that these are cumulative events which are treated as singular, individual incidents. The only continuous factor is that the complainer is seen as a moaner or troublemaker. If the complainer then retaliated at some time they found that they had already been cast as the villain.

Another factor which works against students feeling that they are operating in a just system, stems from schools implementing systems which they believe are fair. What happens in the classroom tends not to follow a student into the playground — dinner supervisors are not told that, say, two children were not getting on in the science or maths lesson. Equally, supervisors do not necessarily pass on details of playground behaviour to class teachers unless the incident approaches the significant or the appalling. As a consequence, much low-level but constant needling can be part of the undercurrent of playground behaviour and this may act disproportionately on specific groups of students.

Students felt that they had responsibility (monitor system, for example) but no power. Where school councils exist, they can be a positive force and a strength. Such councils need to be truly representative and they need to deal with matters which are of real concern to the students. The basis for decision-making has to be clear and where decisions were not in the gift of the council students appreciated explanation, not a knowing silence from the staff who were present. Proper records of the proceedings are needed, as this gave status to the enterprise — the decision-making and the students' contributions.

In considering the development of a school and its ability to suit the students and to fit them for managing the wider world, the views of even the youngest children have value.

Secondary age students

The predominant themes in discussions were fairness, help from teachers and race issues. As with younger students there is an ability to divide the treatment of self from that of others: 'the school is fair to me and not to my friends — so it isn't fair'.

When talking about being able to turn to someone at school for help about half of the students said that there was no-one in school on whom they could rely — personal friends excepted. A typical comment focused on class activity', if you ask a question and don't understand [the answer] then if you ask them again they say you're trouble'. The curriculum/ pastoral divide in some secondary schools may contribute to this perception. In curriculum terms there is an axiom that every teacher should be a teacher of English. Similarly, all teachers should be offering a presentation of themselves to students which encourages students to take their anxieties to them about subject and non-subject related matters. When it comes to issues of race or equality, issues students need to feel that there is more than one person who cares (and anyway, students don't usually know who the equal opportunities co-ordinator is).

Race was a more clearly defined area for discussion. A few students admitted to calling other racist names but about half the students said that they had been called racist names. Again, the range of name-calling is not simply a black/white thing but takes in any grouping and does not necessarily imply dominance. The racist insult is part of the repertoire of insulting language for all who wish to insult. This is a distinct difference from my own experience; that there is a known currency of racist insult did not imply to the older students that there was a race problem,. The active operation of racism, one group to another, was seen by the older students to be more apparent in the younger year groups in the secondary school. Adolescence and the development of active social lives means that the operation of cliques gradually becomes less formal and rigid. Where students returned to school after GCSE examinations, the response to the question: 'Is race an issue at this school?' was 'Last term, definitely, yes. This year, no. It's now personality'. The GCSE hurdle seems to do two things — it puts the academic hurdle more firmly on the agenda as the main purpose for school and it results in the student groupings of the previous five years being broken down and re-formed — either through the coming of new entrants, enrolment on different courses or departure to further education colleges. Students could re-invent themselves and their relationships. The students felt that teaching staff did the same thing.

So, while the use of racial insults is still a potent weapon increasingly it is managed by individual students and groups who are personally and collectively proud of themselves and of their heritage.

Belonging and background

One of the unexpected features of the discussion was difficulty which students, of all ages, from African-Caribbean backgrounds had in identifying themselves. What is not meant is that they do not know who they are but that none of the given labels seem to fit or fit poorly — 'African, African-Caribbean, Afro-Caribbean, Black British'. And where does the mixed race student fit? In the perennial 'other' section? It has been a puzzle to me that African American people had an appellation which linked them with the past and the present. It seemed to be no accident that 'Afro-Caribbean' links only with the past and does not imply rights or settlement or belonging.

One of the major talking points in discussions which relate to race and cultural identity is the extent to which the school should reflect and celebrate the backgrounds of the students within them. Clearly, this is a simple response as pure reflection is not necessarily fertile ground for growth. And celebration required understanding and knowledge to avoid tokenism. The wrong message may be conveyed by schools which try to identify with the backgrounds of students. There continues to be the conceptual leap approach which gives little thought to the reality of being black or Asian in Britain today and which denies black and Asian people born in Britain their birthright — insisting instead on only offering them their parents' or their grandparents' histories.

The work which took place in the late 1960s and early 1970s on Black Studies was timely and right. The air of excitement and discovery was almost tangible. Necessary links were being made. Students felt less like abandoned children with no place to go and no history to have. That work on Black History is now part of an ever-increasing canon. Being black or Asian and British is not the same as being Bajan or Bangladeshi. Employment prospects, education achievement, language repertoire, social groups, status of religion and faith, family structure and even the operation differ from the circumstances of the people who came and who are our parents or our grandparents.

Two cautions — firstly, the danger of denying young, black and ethnic minority people their own history, which is interwoven with the experiences of their white counterparts and secondly, the danger of offering such young people an interpretation of heritage which is obsolete or waning in the birth continues of their parents or grandparents. (On this last issue, a newspaper recently ran a consumer test of a range of woks. Several cooks tested the woks. One white English chef rejected an electric wok on the grounds that, while it performed well it wasn't 'authentic', while a Korean chef said that the electric wok was his first choice because 'that's what we all use at home').

Schools which make concerted efforts to raise the profile of the cultural heritage of students could do worse than asking the students what is best to be done.

A response

This discussion has touched on self-esteem, respect, achievement and circumstances for personal growth. These are central concerns for those of us who work with and for young people. A variety of strategies have been devised to help young people to become the best versions of themselves that they can be. Our school-leavers should increasingly have as part of their life kit a sense of direction, a healthy regard for themselves and others and a feeling that they are only at the beginning of a great and worthwhile adventure.

Mentoring is a strategy which has the potential to help students to develop the skills outlined above. It also offers them experiences which may cause them to re-assess their own worth. A mentor is a guide or an adviser. The mentor takes the role of a constructive, empathetic and focused good acquaintance. When a mentoring partnership is formed, the mentor is clearly identified as having a constructive and supporting role. The other partner, the mentee, could be seen as the active learner. Both are concerned with the development of potential.

Mentoring is an area which is developing in the education field. Whatever the partnerships identified for the mentoring activity, the aim is similar: to use the experience of one person to assist another in making decisions and making sense of their world. To do this clear task-related links are made and friendly working relationships are an essential part of the package.

The year 10 project focused on this age group as the predominant concerns were on enhancing the students achievement and their self esteem. Consequently, the links with black professionals as mentors and role models needed to be effected in time for changes in the student's personal outlook and career direction to be reflected in attitudes to school and in the application to classwork which had the potential to result in higher achievement.

The school was fortunate in having a headteacher who was prepared to give status to the project by his support, a governing body which recognised the need for such an initiative and, importantly, the active support of a group of staff in the school. This group had high profile representation of black women teachers of all levels of seniority within the school. Other staff gave much active and tacit support.

Mentors were enlisted through staff contacts and represented many areas of professional life. All were black. A management committee with representative from the school, business, industry and other interested parties was set up. A co-ordinator was identified from amongst the staff and set about the process of matching mentor to mentee, organising joint meetings of all mentoring partnerships for talks by prominent black people, organising and accompanying the mentees on educational visits and so on. Additionally, she had to develop links with a wide range of benevolent bodies, attempt to fund raise and lead the management of the administrative tasks which surrounded the project.

Issues arose — some able to be solved easily, some less so. A development plan was written, meeting dates for a year ahead were identified. A logo for the project was devised and handbooks were written which described the project to mentors and mentees and which acted as a log to meetings and developments. Discussions were held about the legal responsibility of the school and the mentees' physical and personal well-being. A Code of Conduct for mentors was drawn up. Advice was taken on disclosure and the possible future need to consider specialised support from a counsellor.

The project ended its first year as a considerable success in terms of stronger links being formed between the school and the professional black community. Individual students had good, caring support from people who had 'made it'. The students had been given special time — the high profile launch, articles in newspapers and journals, evening meetings with mentors, an appearance on television which had black presenters who were part of an agenda to widen students horizons. Parents were involved and informed at all stages, which assisted in the further enhancement of the community image of the school.

There were difficulties — and one was centrally concerned with the operation of equal opportunities. Should a school target some of its students for special support? If it does, and the initiative work, can it be denied from other students even 'though the need of others is not as pressing? If the school wishes to manage the project as an associated enterprise and not an integral part of the school, how then are finances managed? How is the time of the co-ordinator, and of other staff accounted for when working on the project? Where does responsibility for the health, safety and welfare of the students on the project lie if an integral part of the project is the development of relationships which reach outside of the school?

Mentoring has the potential to be a valuable took in helping black and ethnic minority students to play a full part in school and wider society.

Conclusion

We have spent time considering young peoples' needs. We understand that there are a range of ways in which we, as educators, may affect the quality of life of our students. In doing so we are likely to improve the quality of school itself.

An important part of the making of a mature person is the ability to recognise what is me and what is not me. In the discussion of race and cultural diversity we need to recognise the pressures and effects of our society on the individual student and on the student as part of the group. In school we also need to recognise the existence of the microcosm. We need to work to realise the worth of the individual in the context of their actual cultural milieu. We need to allow them their own histories with the expectation that they will be enabled to develop their own histories.

Structural aspects of school are crucial in the development of a just society people with mentally healthy citizens. The active planning for an implementation of aims to practice is essential.

Acknowledgements to:

Carmen Rodney, for showing me what hard work and dedication actually mean, in practice. Barbara Sandiford, for a chance conversation which broke the block and re-affirmed the thought. Jerusha Lyseight-jones, for patience and clear thought and for being an authentic voice, and, most importantly, all the young people who gave me time to talk with them.

Notes

1. The questions come from the Technical Paper, 13, 'Schools requiring special measures', *Handbook for the Inspection of Schools*, OFSTED, 1994. The commentary is mine.

2. 'The Eye of the Storm' first shown on BBC in the 1960s.

3. 'A Class Divided' shown on BB2 in 1986. Both available from Concorde Films.

4,5. There are numerous good tests in this area but one which has worked very successfully in a range of schools and environments is *School is us* (WWF./DEP, 1993)

6. This statement does not preclude the possibility that students may have English as an additional language *and* special educational needs — but the terms are not synonymous.

7. OFSTED (1994) *Educational Support for Minority Ethnic Communities*.

8. This work has been developed and promoted by educational consultant, Jenny Moseley. A useful resource is her book 'Turn Your School Around: Circle Time approach to the development of self esteem and positive behaviour in the Primary Staff Room, Classroom and Playground Learning Development Aids ISBN 185503 174 4. Another useful resource is 'Lets Co-operate (Mildred Masheder, 1989, published by the Peace Education Project.

9. A useful text is *The School Effect: a study of multi-racial comprehensives* by David Smith and Sally Tomlinson, Policy Studies Institute, 1989)

10. The paper, *The First Fifty: Equality Assurance and the Inspection of Schools:* a study of 50 of the first 56 reports to be published, with particular attention to how they treat the theory and practice of equality of opportunity' was prepared by the Runnymede Trust as a resource for the conference on 28th June 1994 on 'Equality Assurance and the Inspection of Schools'. The whole report is important reading.

11. For example, *Countering Bullying*, edited by Delwyn Tattum and Graham Herbert. Trentham Books, 1992.

Chapter 4

Towards some understandings of sexuality education

Brenda Hanson and Paul Patrick

The issue of sex education is one that is frequently surrounded by controversy and confusion. In this chapter we take a look at the legislation and guidelines provided by central government and at how a school can develop a positive approach that caters for the needs of all pupils and gives parents an understanding of the issues raised and the context in which they occur.

The national and political context

On 6th May 1994, the Department for Education issued Circular 5/94, which sets out the statutory position on sex education in schools, following the changes introduced by the Education Act 1993 which came into force on 1st September 1994. This circular states that the Government 'believes that all pupils should be offered the opportunity of receiving a comprehensive, well-planned programme of sex education during their school careers.' This, they believe, will fulfil the requirement of section 1 of the Education Reform Act 1988 which states that the school curriculum should be one which 'promotes the spiritual, moral, cultural, mental and physical development of pupils' and 'prepares such pupils for the opportunities, responsibilities and experiences of adult life.'

Such a statement may be greeted with some surprise by practitioners in the field, coming as it does from a government whose many public pronouncements, particularly by John Patten when Minister for Education, suggested at best an antipathy towards any form of sex education in schools. There is, in our view, a clear dichotomy between the public statements of the politicians, whose aims are to please the constituency they serve, and actual policy. It would therefore be useful to move away from the circus that passes for political debate in this area and to look briefly at both the legal constraints and the additional guidelines that have been provided to facilitate interpretation of the law.

In 1986 and 1987 the government published two documents which 'have been instrumental in influencing how schools should teach sex education' (Taylor and Brierley). The first was the Education Act, (No.2) 1986, which put sex education 'within a legal framework' and this was followed by the Department of Education and Science (DES) Circular No. 11/87 which gave further guidance to educational bodies following the establishment of the 1986 Act. The major change brought about by this legislation was to hand responsibility to the governing bodies of schools for determining 'if, and in what way' sex education should be part of the secular curriculum . It was the same Act that determined a restructuring of the governing bodies of schools with the particular effect of increasing parental representation.

Much was made at the time of the suggestion that certain education authorities, particularly those, like the Inner London Education Authority, who had 'progressive' reputations, were pursuing a 'left-wing' agenda of which most parents disapproved. It was in the field of sex education generally and the treatment of lesbian and gay sexuality particularly, that this particular case was made most frequently. For those of us working in the field of sex education at the time, it was clear that the government thought that the increased participation of parents in the decision- making process surrounding sex education issues would curb what were considered to be the excesses currently practiced in the field. Parental 'opinion' frequently being used to justify the government's ideological interventions in this area. It was a miscalculation. Whilst parents had, and continue to have many concerns about sex education, the vast majority remain staunchly in favour and wish it to cover the full range of human sexuality and to explore the complex social and moral issues that arise from it.

Far from restricting the practice of sex education in schools, the legislation created new and much-needed forums for debate that brought new life to this area of the curriculum. Even though it did not make it mandatory for sex education to be included in the school curriculum, the Act did encourage heads, teachers and governors, with strong parental participation, to formulate new sex education policies and to evaluate and revise existing ones. It also, somewhat ironically, increased local education authority involvement in the establishing of policy and practice, as many governing bodies and schools turned to their authorities for advice and guidance. Such a shot in the arm was sorely necessary because what had been taught earlier was known to be patchy in quality and quantity'.

A survey of health education policies in schools conducted by the National Foundation for Educational Research and the Health Education Authority, found that by 1992, 54% of primary schools and 82% of secondary schools had a written policy for teaching sex education and that 12% of primary schools and 1% of secondary had made the policy decision to exclude sex education from their curriculum.

Section 28

The next major intervention by government into the legislation surrounding sex education came not from the then Department of Education and Science but from a private member's bill that was then accepted by government into the Local Government Bill of 1988. This was the notorious Section 28, which states 'A local authority shall not... promote the teaching in any maintained school of the acceptability of homosexuality as a pretended family relationship.' The section became law on a wave of misinformation, half-truth, prejudice and tabloid hype.

The proposers of the section, particularly David Wiltshire, Gill Knight and Michael Howard asserted that there were schools, entirely, it transpired, in education authorities run by Labour, who were abusing their position by 'promoting' homosexuality amongst their pupils. On no occasion was any such school named or any evidence provided on how this had been achieved. In fact Haringey Education Authority, which was considered to be the major villain of the piece, had merely suggested that as part of schools' equal opportunities education the position of young lesbians and gay men should be taken into account but that under no circumstances should any such initiative be taken without full consultation with parents. At the time of the passing of Section 28 into law, no such initiative had been undertaken in any Haringey school.

The party political, rather than educational, nature of the debate can clearly be seen from the text of an advertisement which ran in national newspapers at the time of the local elections. Beneath a photograph of a Haringey woman and her children ran the words:

> My name is Betty Sheridan. I live in Haringey. I'm a mother with two kids and I'm scared. If you vote Labour they will teach my kids about gays and lesbians instead of giving them a proper education.

What the advertisement declined to tell us was that Mrs Sheridan was a Roman Catholic who sent her children to Roman Catholic schools over which Haringey Education Authority had no jurisdiction in this area.

(For further information on the scapegoating of Haringey Education Authority see 'Positive Images in Haringey — *A Struggle for Identity* by D. Cooper, in *Learning Our Lines — Sexuality and Social Control in Education*, edited by Carol Jones and Pat Mahoney, Women's Press 1989.)

However the fact that Section 28 was remarkably loosely worded, lacking any concrete meaning — how do you promote homosexuality?- and completely unnecessary, since the excesses it was designed to curb were never proven to exist, it still became law and had what many believe to be its intended effect. This was to pass a warning shot across the bows of all schools and local education authorities who desired to develop a sex education policy and practice that serves the needs of all the members of their communities. Its implications went deeper than the treatment of lesbian and gay sexuality in schools, raising yet again the spectre of schools encouraging immorality and denying parental wishes in the teaching in this area. That the arguments put forward ran counter to the guidance provided by government through its own guidelines on sex education, simply illustrates the confusion that is created when sound educational practice runs counter to the political agendas of individual politicians and governments.

There are many examples of this occurring. Despite clear public support by government for comprehensive sex education, as shown at the beginning of this chapter, there are many who proclaim a different view and will use their position to create the very confusion that concerns many parents and teachers and sometimes prevents the development of good practice based on sound educational research. Take James Pawsey, Conservative MP for Rugby and Kenilworth, who wrote

> Despite the growing emphasis on teaching of sex, the rate of abortions continues to increase, and small wonder, for if we teach our children German, can we be surprised if they practice it.

That such a bizarre remark flies in the face of all research done in the area seems not to bother Mr Pawsey in the least. As is so frequently the case in discussions of this topic, the personal political agenda is more important than factual accuracy. To put the record straight, Saskia Bellman, writing in the *Guardian* in November 1993, compares the approach to sex education in Britain with that in the Netherlands. She states that Dutch young people 'are bombarded with sex education, yet teenage pregnancies in the Netherlands are the lowest in the Western world and teenage abortion rates are ten times lower than in Britain.' She adds that attitudes to the range of human sexuality are far more open and positive. She also notes with some incredulity, that 'Britain, with the highest teenage pregnancy rate in Europe, has just given parents the right to exempt their children from a school's sex education programme.'

Banning Health Education Authority sex education materials

The confusion that surrounds policy in this area continues to spread. One recent example was the banning by Brian Mawhinney, Health Minister, of a book prepared by the Health Education Authority. This was done even though many educationalists and organisations who work with young people thought that it was an excellent, educative and accessible publication. It is the opinion of the authors of this chapter that it was a very useful addition to resources for sex education and that it certainly fulfilled the government's criteria, quoted earlier, in that it 'promotes the spiritual, moral, cultural, mental and physical development' of young people.

This booklet, *Your Pocket Guide to Sex,* written by Nick Fisher, the 'agony uncle' for 'Just 17' magazine has since been published by Penguin. It was aimed at 16 to 26 year olds and covered such topics as contraception, HIV, safer sex, the range of human sexuality and also discussed the emotional, moral social and political contexts in which they occur. Even so, Mr Mawhinney found it 'inappropriate, distasteful and smutty' and thousands of copies were pulped. Yet another case of a political agenda overriding the educational needs of young people. Your authors can only concur with Nick Fisher when he stated, on hearing of the ban, that: 'I don't believe this government has teenagers' interests at heart.'

1993 Education Act

The next Government move in this area was the introduction of the Education Act 1993, section 241 of which states that sex education must be provided to all registered pupils in maintained secondary schools, whilst also providing parents, for the first time, with the statutory right to remove their children from all or part of the sex education provided. It also stated that such sex education must include information on sexually transmitted diseases, HIV and AIDS. These topics also formed a compulsory part of the National Curriculum in Science and therefore became part of every pupil's secondary education. However, in the summer of 1994, bowing to political pressure against the weight of very strong educational opinion, the Secretary of State for Education made an order to remove any materials on sexually transmitted diseases, HIV and AIDS' from the compulsory science curriculum, leaving it only within the sex education programme from which pupils may be withdrawn. We believe that such an act could result in children not being given vital life-saving information from any part of the curriculum. Thus, what may be seen as progressive legislation, in so far as it insists that all secondary schools provide sex education courses for their pupils, has a clause built into it which could have devastating consequences for some pupils.

David Brindle, the Social Services Correspondent for the *Guardian,* attended the public health doctors' conference in London and wrote on June 15th 1994:

Teenagers will be put at risk by the Government's policy on sex education in schools, public health doctors warned yesterday. Guidelines coming into force in September would allow parents to withdraw their children from sex education classes which would be their only opportunity to be taught about contraception, HIV, and AIDS', the doctors said.

He continues:

Science lessons about reproduction, genetics and infertility will remain compulsory. But contraception and sexual health issues will be raised in sex education lessons, which all state secondary schools must offer but which pupils will only attend with their parents' consent.' Doctors at the conference passed a resolution warning that the guidelines 'would not promote the health of schoolchildren and would run counter to the Government's Health of the Nation strategy, aiming to| curb teenage pregnancies and the spread of AIDS.'

The Government's White Paper — *The Health of the Nation* — was published in July 1992. It identifies sexual health as one of the five key areas in which a substantial improvement in health could be achieved. The White Paper set a number of objectives and targets, including a 50% reduction in the rate of pregnancies among the under 16s by the year 2000. Another target is to lessen the incidence of HIV, AIDS' and other sexually transmitted diseases. Circular 5/94 states that education has a vital part to play in achieving these and other *Health of the Nation* targets and that sex education, taught within a clear moral framework, can make a substantial contribution.

That the issue of sex education should raise so many contradictions in policy should come as little surprise. It is an issue that has always excited a wide range of personal viewpoints, touching as it does on so many moral, religious social and political agendas of so many individuals and groups. However, it is the job of the school, through its governing body, parents and teachers, to set a curriculum that meets the needs of all its pupils and is reliant upon established research and good practice rather than a set of personal ideologies. There is much in law and in the guidance provided by government and other bodies that can be helpful, once it has been reviewed in a proper educational context .

Few could disagree with the quote at the beginning of this chapter from Government circular 5/94 and, whilst individual interventions have intentionally attempted to cloud the issues, we now know that Section 28 of the Local Government Act has no affect whatsoever on any school's curriculum (For further information see: *Section 28; A Guide for Schools, Teachers and Governors* (1989) London ALTARF, and 'Section 28 and Education' by S. Sanders and G. Spraggs (1989) in *Learning Our Lines — Sexuality and Social Control in Education* edited by Carol Jones and Pat Mahoney, Women's Press.) It is real progress that sex education must by law be provided in all secondary schools, a provision that should now be extended to the primary sector.

The legal right of parents to remove their children from all or part of a sex education programme is, as has been pointed out, a retrograde step. Yet we have found that where a school works closely with its parents in the development of sex education, encouraging in them an understanding of both the content and process of the work and seeking their active participation, such a veto is rarely if ever used. Whilst there are certainly more appropriate ways to encourage schools to work closely with parents, the right of parents to remove their children from aspects of this work does highlight the essential need to prevent this happening. Nor should this be viewed as a particular difficulty. Isobel Allen's research (1987) into parental attitudes to sex education found that 96% of parents felt that schools should teach sex education and the vast majority of the rest had no opinion for or against.

Sex Education or Sexuality Education

We have summarised the confusion that exists in the current government position on sex education and suggested that there is nothing in either legislation or guidance to prevent effective sex education being provided in our schools. Schools must be prepared to take their parents along with them, by giving meaning to the term 'sex education' and clarifying what such a curriculum could look like.

David Brierley and Neil Taylor (1992) also reflect upon the many agendas, used to define what sex education should be and find that 'considerable problems arise even in trying to define the term.' Dorothy Dallas (1972) argues that sex education:

is a wide, all-embracing and all but meaningless term; various synonyms have been coined and employed, but have failed to replace it in common usage... It's interpretation has been sharply polarised; on the one hand it is associated with anatomical diagrams and bald explanations of physiological processes, while on the other the vaguer realms of 'personal relationships are explored.

The two extremes defined by Dallas are, we're certain, easily recognisable. However it is our experience that what Ms Dallas somewhat dismissively refers to as 'the vaguer realms of personal relationships' is the context in which all this work, physiological or attitudinal, should take place. A more positive definition comes from the Family Planning Association (1988) who point out that sex education is about helping children and young people relate to other people, 'respecting the rights and feelings of others, developing loving, caring relationships as friends, parents, members of a family and sexual partners'. It also involves 'learning to say 'no' to unwanted sexual advances, and how to protect oneself from abuse and exploitation.'

Clearly such empowerment cannot be developed simply through the amassing of information, although factual knowledge about people's bodies, contraception, the practical aspects of sexual enjoyment, reproduction and sexually transmitted diseases is an essential part of the development of such confidence. It is therefore clear that in its widest interpretation, all teachers have a role to play in sex education as they encourage children to seek the positive in themselves and relate positively to others. The effectiveness of such work will be heavily dependent on the ethos of a school and the relationships that occur between teacher and pupil, pupil and pupil, teacher and teacher and school and parents. Without a positive context it would be difficult to see such sensitive work being successful. Such an ethos must be informed by an active policy commitment to equal opportunities. The authors are fortunate to work in a school that commits itself to equality for all and seeks to give equal treatment, both in its day-to-day running and through the curriculum, to all individuals and groups that it serves. In the context of sex education these include women, lesbians and gay men, people with HIV and AIDS', whilst respecting the range of cultural and religious values within the school. Such a commitment will never be perfect and will always throw up a range of contradictions, but it is our belief that such a background is an essential base for this work.

Throughout this chapter we have used the term 'sex education' and, like Dorothy Dallas (1972), we have some problems with it. It seems to us to emphasise the physiological aspects of the issue, suggesting acts rather than attitude, information without empowerment. That is clearly what it meant to James Pawsey, the MP quoted earlier. Whilst misconceptions about sex education abound, we think that the term itself exacerbates them. We much prefer the term 'sexuality education', which to us suggests the wider issues involved and the moral, social and political contexts in which they should be viewed. It acknowledges that this work is not simply about plumbing and how it works but about whole persons and their relationship with the world.

Further, we would like to suggest that basing sexuality education on the biological aspects of reproduction distorts a proper understanding of human sexuality and its complexity. It is very easy for young people who have been told that sex is for reproduction to look upon other forms of sexual expression from masturbation, foreplay, non-penetrative sex to lesbian and gay sex as 'unnatural', and to consider themselves not completely human if they either not to have children or are unable to do so. It also gives a primacy to the male orgasm at the expense of the wide range of physical and emotional pleasures that can be derived from the various forms of sexual expression.

Sexuality education should be based in the person — their feelings, confusions, pleasures, self-image as well as their physiology. It should, as is made clear by 'Reynold Jones (1989), discuss what is important to young people today. At its sharpest point it must, to quote Carol Lee (1988), be 'the alleviation of dreads', but it must further, to provide all young people with an understanding of their sexuality, the choices that flow from it and the knowledge, understandings and power to make those choices positive, responsible and informed.

An approach to sexuality education

So, what are the elements that may make up such a programme and where could cross-curricular links be developed? We have already stressed the need for presenting the range of human sexuality — heterosexual, lesbian, gay and bisexual — in a manner that allows young people to see them as part of ordinary human experience. This is something that, in our experience, needs continual reinforcement, given that in our society all people are assumed to be heterosexual until proven differently (and even then the notion that ordinary people could be lesbian, gay or bisexual is sufficiently problematic for some people to create elaborate processes of denial). It is a role of the sexuality educator to bring young people back to the reality of the range of human sexuality, through both the resources presented and their own interaction with the group. This can be a difficult process and needs proper planning and discussion with other staff if it is to succeed.

Careful thought will need to be given to the teacher's response to the inevitable question 'Are you gay/lesbian /bisexual?' This may be of particular importance for staff whose honest response could leave them vulnerable. As with other sensitive areas, we believe that there is a need for whole school guidelines so that individual teachers do not feel at risk. (For further discussion see 'Are you a lesbian Miss?' by Sanders and Burke, (1994) and Patrick and Burke (1993).

Sadly, when taking such an approach, teachers will discover a paucity of materials available to support it and may well need to create appropriate materials for themselves. However these need not be too complex as, in our experience, simple trigger materials can create lengthy, stimulating and rewarding discussion.

Creating a safe learning environment

The forum for such discussion is also important. We feel that in a mixed school it is essential that single sex groupings are organised, taken by a staff member of the same gender, particularly in the lower secondary school where such discussions are frequently accompanied by embarrassment, covered by either silence or forced and frequently aggressive jocularity. We also feel that as pupils develop their understandings and feel more comfortable with the issues there should be, where possible, mixed forums for such discussions. As much of the discussion that will take place in such forums will be of a challenging and sensitive nature, it is vitally important that a proper disciplinary structure is created to prevent scapegoating or inappropriate responses from pupils. The balance between creating a sympathetic accessibility and maintaining a controlled environment is a difficult one to achieve and usually only occurs with time. It would be our advice to begin with a clear, firm disciplinary structure.

Thought should also be given to the language that pupils and staff use in discussion of issues of sexuality. There is an argument that says that pupils will feel more comfortable and take greater ownership of a discussion if they are allowed to use the words that they would use more commonly amongst their friends. However teachers must be aware that many of the colloquial words used to describe sexual functions and parts of the body have strongly abusive connotations and will certainly be offensive to some. Language must be negotiated between teacher and pupil so that it is clear what is acceptable and what is not. This should be done at the beginning of a course and regularly reinforced. An investigation into why so many of the common words used to discuss sexuality and sexual practice have abusive connotations, particularly in their attack upon all women's and gay sexuality is a fruitful follow-up to this, and allows a chance for a wide range of attitudes to be examined.

Meeting pupils' needs

Teachers working in sexuality education will also need continually to reappraise the content and practice of their work so that it remains appropriate to the needs of the groups they are teaching. This monitoring of what works and what does not work with particular groups should be a regular agenda item on PHSE group meetings. In individual classrooms, however, we have also found it useful to give pupils space to set their own agendas from time to time. The simplest and, to our mind, most effective method of doing this is to provide each pupil with a piece of paper on which they can raise an issue anonymously. In using this method teachers should make sure that each pupil writes something on the paper so that pupils with valid questions or concerns do not fear peer group intimidation. Suggest to pupils who have nothing to ask or are too anxious to do so, is to write 'I have nothing I want to discuss at the present time' or some such line.

This exercise should take place at the end of a session so the teacher has a chance to analyse the issues that pupils have requested and develop in consultation with colleagues the most appropriate responses. To attempt to answer such questions without preparation runs the risks of losing control, using inappropriate methods of investigation, and the teacher being made vulnerable. Nor should it be assumed that because a topic has not been raised by the group in this way that this means it is irrelevant to their needs. There may, for instance be all sorts of social pressures that stop pupils raising certain issues, even anonymously and they may be the very reasons why that topic needs to be discussed.

Of course, issues of sexuality education do not always occur conveniently in the lessons timetabled for them. It is as likely that the Geography or French teacher will be asked to comment on the lesbian kiss in Brookside or to intervene when a boy refers to a girl as a 'slag'. Again the response will depend to a great degree on the ethos of the school and the relationship between teacher and pupils. Of course the use of sexist language, as with any other form of abuse, must be dealt with immediately and be seen to be done so that it is clearly a disciplinary matter. However, attempts to engage staff in discussion about issues not related to the subject are frequently used by pupils to delay the real work at hand or to make staff uncomfortable. The decision on whether this is a genuine request for discussion/support/advice is always a difficult one and staff with any concerns should insist on pupils returning to the work in hand and then raising the issue with a form tutor, head of year or personal , health, and social education teacher.

Not all requests for discussion or support, however, occur within the classroom. Any member of staff may be taken to one side by a pupil who wishes to discuss something in private, but the very nature of the subject matter of a sexuality education course and the nature of the relationship created between teacher and pupil means that a sexuality educator is often the pupil's first choice. It is, of course, part of any teacher's role to advise and support children where possible. Yet this can cause many concerns when the issues raised are to do with sexuality.

Firstly a teacher will almost certainly be asked for a promise of confidentiality. This cannot be given until the nature of the issue is known.

A teacher has a legal obligation to pass on to the designated member of staff in the school any knowledge, or even suspicion, of abuse, sexual or otherwise. It would therefore be totally wrong to allow a pupil to think they were automatically being given confidentiality. If a teacher receives such a request, it must be pointed out to the pupil that, although there may be many issues that may be discussed confidentially, if the teacher feels that the child is at risk then the information will be passed on. It is important to explain clearly where such information will go and what may happen next. Any teacher unsure of these procedures should, as a matter of urgency, discover who is the designated member of staff and what the procedures are. That member of staff should always be someone with wide experience in this field, who has the confidence of staff, pupils and parents. If this were not to be the case then it is incumbent upon staff to make representations to the Headteacher and if necessary the governing body, so important is this person's role. It is worth noting that however difficult this may be for teachers, it is still on the whole far easier than for either pupils or parents.

The designated member of staff should also be able to provide support to staff who are told about a range of other issues from suspected pregnancy to lesbian or gay sexuality. Such advice may be obtained from any trusted source that knows the teacher and the school well. It is also not necessary for a teacher seeking such advice to name the pupil. What steps are taken from that point on will depend upon the practice and policy of individual schools as negotiated with pupils and parents. Any school that does not have such agreed guidelines risks leaving its staff very vulnerable.

A whole school approach

The nature and content of sexuality education is very wide ranging, taking in as it does the pupil's self-image, the complete range of social interactions in which the pupils are involved, factual information and an understanding of the moral, social, cultural and political context in which the pupils relate. This is clearly a whole school issue. Positive sexuality education can only take place in a context that encourages self- worth and the empowerment of pupils. This will be done through all areas of the curriculum as well as in the day-to-day interaction between teacher and pupil, pupil and pupil, and pupil and home.

There are several areas of the curriculum that obviously lend themselves to the exploration of sexuality education issues — a discursive essay on abortion and many of the studied texts in English, a piece of Drama about whether or not to become sexually active, or a young lesbian or gay man coming out to their family, an exploration of identity through Artwork, a song about relationships in Music are a few obvious examples. However, all subjects have a contribution to make to this work. Particular praise for commitment to a piece of Mathematics work or acknowledgement of extra effort in History is an essential part of the process of empowering young people to feel positive about themselves, which in turn is essential to success in this area.

Another vitally important way a school develops feelings of security and self-worth in pupils is through the active pursual of equal opportunities throughout the school. All pupils and staff must feel confident that issues of racial, sexual, anti-gay and anti-lesbian harassment, bullying and all other forms of intimidation are taken seriously and properly dealt with. Further, it is important that schools see as a cause for celebration the diversity of both the school community and the wider world that surrounds it. This can be done in many ways from day to day interaction to whole school celebrations. The authors work in a school where, over the past few years, there have been full school assemblies led by the Headteacher and involving pupils, parents, teaching and support staff, governors and outside speakers, to mark such occasions as International Women's Day, Nelson Mandela's release from prison and later free elections in South Africa, Martin Luther King's birthday, May Day, Lesbian and Gay Pride Week and World AIDS' Day — all accompanied by appropriate displays including pupils' own work, much of which was initiated within the Personal, Health and Social Education Programme.

Cross-curricular approaches are frequently considered time-consuming and difficult to achieve, particularly now, when there are so many additional demands upon teachers. However we maintain that such an approach is essential to the provision of sexuality education. Nor need it be particularly problematic. It is dependent upon a clearly written and detailed sexuality education policy which, besides being a legal necessity, is a baseline from which a mapping exercise can be done to discover what curriculum areas are already offering to pupils. From there it is not a great task for the personal, health and social education team to fill any gaps that may show themselves.

Whilst we believe firmly in the importance of a cross-curricular approach in this area, we also acknowledge the centrality of a specialist team headed by a PHSE Co-ordinator to teach aspects of the course that other staff may be unwilling or lacking in confidence to teach. How such a division of content can be achieved would differ from school to school. It is also essential in our view that such a team meet regularly to discuss their responses to what will frequently be difficult questions and intractable attitudes.

Involving parents

Working with parents — always important but, because of the legal situation discussed earlier, now essential — also needs careful thought and should be defined by a whole-school approach rather than through individual contact that can put undue pressure on staff and lead to misunderstanding. Sexuality education raises many concerns for parents, particularly when our tabloid press distorts and sensationalises its practice on a regular basis. It is the duty of schools to respond to these concerns in a forthright manner based on educational principles. Parents must feel they have access to the curriculum and an understanding of the importance of the topics covered and range of strategies used in the classroom. Schools too often take a defensive approach, shying away from those topics that they feel parents may consider difficult. In our view such an approach is based upon frequently misplaced assumptions of parental wishes and a disregard for the needs of pupils. However we do feel that in involving parents it is necessary to give them an overview of the aims and objectives of the whole course so that any individual unit of work that raises concerns may be put into its full educational context.

We suggest, this can be most effectively achieved through a regularly timetabled meeting of a Parent/Staff Association that reviews the school's sexuality education policy and examines the resources and methods of working used to achieve the agreed aims. Such a meeting should be part of a series of meetings that give parents access to all areas of the curriculum. To provide this opportunity for the examination of the sexuality curriculum alone could suggest areas of controversy that may not exist. However, occasionally, such discussions will be pre-empted by a parent expressing concern to the school about a unit of work currently being taught. Clearly the school must respond to such concerns but the same guidelines should apply. The response should not come from the teacher who is teaching the course but from the PHSE Co-ordinator or member of the Senior Management Team and should be discussed in the context of agreed school policy and the wider educational approach.

When a parent contacted the Headteacher of a secondary school to express concern over the showing of a video on the experiences of young lesbians and gay men within a sexuality education unit, she was invited into the school by the PHSE Co-ordinator to look at the whole programme of work of which this lesson was a part. It was explained how the work fitted with the school's sexuality education and equal opportunities policies, to which she had agreed when her children were admitted to the school and only then, once context had been clearly explained, was she shown the video that had caused the concern. Whilst such an approach is time-consuming and cannot always guarantee success, it does allow parents to make an informed judgement on this part of their children's education and where that occurs it is our experience, as in this case, that results are almost always positive.

To summarise, sexuality education forms an essential part of any child's development to adulthood. It has recently been somewhat regulated by National Government and sensationalised by the tabloid press. Yet with the correct approach there is nothing to prevent schools from developing a curriculum that responds to pupils' needs and raises with them a range of issues that are at the heart of what it is to be human. Sexuality is a topic that excites us all and is a cause of frequent discussion, anxiety and joy. It is up to schools to decide whether that discussion takes place within the structured and secure environment of the classroom, where fears can be allayed and informed opinion developed, or in the playground where fear and ignorance frequently rule.

References

Allen, Isobel (1987) *Education in Sex and Personal Relationships.* Policy Studies Institute

ALTARF (1989) *Section 28; a Guide for Schools, Teachers and Governors.* London, ALTARF

Brierley, David and Taylor, Neil (1992) 'The impact of the Law on the Development of a Sex Education Programme at a Leicestershire Comprehensive School', in *Pastoral Care*, March

Dallas, Dorothy M. (1972) Sex Education in School and Society. NFER

Family Planning Association (1988) *Sex Education in Schools: A Leaflet for Parents and Governors.* FPA

Jones, Reynolds (1989) *Sex Education in Personal and Social Education.* Kogan Page

Lee, Carol (1988) *Friday's Child: The Threat to Moral Education.* Wellingborough, Thonsons

Patrick, P. and Burke, H. (1993) 'Equal Opportunities and Sexuality' in *Equality Matters* edited by Hilary Claire, Janet Maybin and Joan Swann. Avon, Multilingual Matters

Sanders, S. and Burke, H. (1994) 'Are you a lesbian Miss', in *Challenging Lesbian and Gay inequalities in education.* Open University Press

Sanders, S. and Spraggs, G. (1989) 'Section 28 and education', in *Learning our lines — sexuality and social control in education* edited by Carol Jones and Pat Mahoney. London, Women's Press

---
Chapter 5

Citizenship education — more than a forgotten cross curricular theme?

Martin Buck and Sally Inman

In chapter 1 we discussed what we might mean by pupils' personal development and suggested a framework to plan curriculum provision which would explicitly foster that development in pupils. We argued that the cross-curricular elements — the themes, dimensions and skills — should remain central to that provision regardless of the apparent silence of the Schools Curriculum and Assessment Authority (SCAA) over their future status within the curriculum. In this chapter we focus on citizenship education as an example of a cross-curricular theme whose breadth encompasses issues and concerns not just for the taught curriculum but also for the whole school. We discuss models of citizenship education and argue for a model which McGoughlin (1992) has called maximalist — radical in intent and permeating all aspects of school life. We then return to the framework described in Chapter 1 and demonstrate how that can help us to plan and implement citizenship education within the taught curriculum. We use two case studies drawn from the primary curriculum — *Ourselves* and *Food and Sustainability.*

Citizenship education — the whole curriculum context

Before we look at citizenship education it is necessary to review the purpose and nature of the five cross-curricular themes within the curriculum. In the original guidance from the then National Curriculum Council, the themes were described as having a particular nature and purpose. The NCC Circular 6 made clear that the themes were designed to make an important contribution:

Themes contribute to personal and social development in a number of ways.

- They explore the values and beliefs which influence the individual and his or her relationship with others and the wider world.

- They help pupils to respond to their present lives and prepare them for work and adult life.

- They emphasise practical activities, decision making,learning through experience, and the development of close links between the school and the wider world.

- They provide relevant ways in which skills might be developed (NCC, 1990).

However, from the beginning there were difficulties about the role and importance of the cross-curricular themes. The choice of the particular themes by the NCC was presented as self-evident, they were somehow the 'obviously' appropriate cross-curricular areas. No real rationale was given as to why these had been identified rather than other themes. Much of the NCCC guidance lacked coherence and rigour, both within and across the themes.

Despite these problems, however, the themes provided a genuine opportunity to extend and enhance the curriculum for pupils. The opportunities would have been strengthened had the themes been set within a coherent framework in which values were made explicit at a whole curriculum level. The themes themselves provided such opportunities. Within, for example, health education, environmental education and citizenship education there are more radical perspectives which take the themes into the whole school and begin to ask some fundamental questions, not just about the curriculum but also about the nature of the institution itself. Health education can be limited to a formal health education curriculum but can also be viewed as an integral part of a whole school approach to health. Similarly, environmental education at its broadest is part of a wider concern for education for sustainability in which questions are raised about how the school operates from day to day.

Education for citizenship can remain at the level of taught curriculum or it can encompass a whole school commitment to the development of young citizens. This latter approach would include a fundamental review of the structures and relationships within the institution alongside the taught curriculum provision. Economic and Industrial Understanding (EIU) has the capacity to make a link between the curriculum and whole school practice; some of the TVEI and SCIP inspired initiatives have demonstrated such a capacity within, for example, enterprise awareness projects. We should also recognise that notions of a health-promoting school or a school committed to sustainability will be premised on conceptions of economic understanding which will need expurgating.

Careers education and guidance has perhaps a weaker claim to a whole institutional perspective. Careers Education and Guidance would seem to lack the conceptual framework needed to enable it to have a broader institutional view. However, the personal and social skills promoted through careers education and guidance should permeate all aspects of school life and thus this part of Careers Education and Guidance has a generic quality.

When the themes are viewed in this way, their importance to pupils' personal development becomes greater. Each has a similar message in terms of a whole-school approach encompassing taught curriculum provision through personal, social and health education (PSHE), subjects, thematic work alongside wider aspects of schooling such as assemblies, circle time, extra-curricular activities and voluntary work. These would be set within the context of explicit and agreed school values and ethos.

What then of the cross-curricular dimensions and skills? The focus of this chapter is with citizenship education as a cross curricular theme but the work is predicated on the assumption that all curriculum development within this area must build in precepts which ensure that equal opportunities and multicultural education are visible to curriculum planners and to the learners. Similarly, we are assuming curriculum development which explicitly promotes a range of affective and intellectual skills which also have an equal opportunities and multicultural dimension to them. This curriculum perspective must itself be alive in the day-to-day relations and practices of the institution.

Education for Citizenship

Citizenship education is neither a creation of the ERA nor of the National Curriculum Council but has a long and chequered history. Before and certainly throughout this century there have been versions of citizenship education, variously entitled: civics, political studies, world studies, social education, general studies, PSHE. The role and purpose of citizenship education has varied according to the dominant concerns of any time. Alongside the formal taught provision there has been an equally long tradition of broader curriculum provision embedded within, for example school councils, community and voluntary work, circle time, assemblies etc. This chapter will not attempt to review this history, others have already done this in some detail (eg. Brown, 1991). We will limit ourselves to a brief discussion of some of the pushes for citizenship education in the 1980s and 1990s.

The 1980s and 1990s

In the mid-1980s a new push for citizenship education came from a number of sources: The Swann Report of 1985 argued for its inclusion on the grounds that

> A good education must give every youngster the knowledge, under-standing and skills to function effectively as an individual and as a citizen in a wider national society and in the world community of which he or she is also a member.

Perhaps the most significant influence was the Speakers Commission on Citizenship Education of 1990. Bernard Weatherill made his view clear:

> 'I believe that citizenship, like anything else has to be learned. Young people do not become good citizens by accident... '

In its unpublished report, the Commission declared:

> The Commission strongly supports the case for citizenship studies to be a part of every young person's education whether in state or private sector schools, irrespective of the course of study being followed, and

from the earliest years of schooling and continuing into the post school years within further and higher education and the youth service (1990).

The NCC seemed to affirm this view and citizen education was included as one of the five cross-curricular themes of the new curriculum. In the foreword to Curriculum Guidance 8, Duncan Graham said 'Education for citizenship is essential for every pupil'.. The introduction quotes the then Secretary of State arguing for citizenship education as essential to the fulfilment of the aims of ERA.

Education should and must develop pupils'potential to the full and prepare them for the world in which they live. This was underlined by the Secretary for State for Education and Science who, in a speech give to the National Conference on citizenship in Schools in February 1990 said that 'unless citizenship forms a part of what schools seek to convey to their pupils, the aims as set out in the Act will not be achieved (NCC, 1990).

The National Commission on Education published its report, *Learning to Succeed,* in 1993. It declared that:'We consider the teaching of citizenship of great importance' and outlined the essential elements of effective citizenship education.

What kind of citizenship education do we want?

Although we might agree on the need for citizenship education, this could be for very different reasons since there are different models and each has a view, explicit or implicit, of what it is (and often what it should be) to be a citizen. This chapter is not the place to review the long and complex political and philosophical debates on citizenship — debates that have been around for centuries. Suffice it to say that the term citizenship has always been open to conflicting meanings — throughout history there have been conflicting definitions of critical strands of citizenship, such as who belongs, to what they belong, and what it means to belong. These differences can be seen both between and within conventional 'right' and 'left' political thinking.

However, within all these debates we can detect, albeit in very crude terms, differences of opinion around a limited number of what we might describe as the essential areas of citizenship. Hall and Held (1989) have described these essential areas as: membership; rights and duties; and participation in practice. Within each of these areas of citizenship we have what Mcloughlin (1992) has described as a minimalist and maximalist view of citizenship.

i. A minimalist view of membership would see membership of society in terms of a formal and legal status, often bestowed by the state and involving such things as having a passport or voting rights. A maximalist notion of membership would involve a sense of real equality and justice for everyone and a conception of identity as one which is central to citizenship and which is recognised as both individual and cultural.

ii. A minimalist version of rights and duties is concerned with formal rights but has an emphasis on public duty, whilst a maximalist version would put rights and duties in the context of a wider understanding of cultural and social inequalities.

iii. A minimalist view of participation would be restricted to notions of representation, voting and pressure group politics, whilst a more maximalist view would see citizens as being fully engaged in all decisions affecting their lives.

So there are significant issues about how we understand citizenship. There are equally important and related issues to do with the geographical boundaries of our citizenship — specifically whether our citizenship remains confined to a nation state or extends to Europe and world citizenship.

Models of citizenship education

These different models of citizenship underpin the different models of citizenship education, and so the latter too, falls crudely into minimalist and maximalist. The minimalist model of citizenship education is largely concerned with: the provision of information about society; and with the socialisation of young people into a given and often taken-for-granted society. Such a model stresses duties and responsibilities and has little concern for developing pupils' critical powers. At one extreme such an education is concerned to produce what some have described as ' new moral soldiers' or 'active citizens in uniform'. This extreme minimalist conception is best epitomised by Douglas Hurd's view that citizenship education would help young people to: 'take an interest in their community and help us restore the amazing social cohesion of Victorian England' (*The Guardian*, 9.11.1988).)

A maximalist conception of citizenship, education is concerned with empowerment, with developing pupils ability to take control and exercise responsibility over their own lives. It involves the development of pupils' ability to ask critical questions, evaluate evidence, question the taken-for-granted. It aims to develop personal self-awareness and understanding and knowledge and also understanding on a wider societal and global level. This conception of citizenship education is concerned equally with content and with learning processes and is perhaps best summed up by Manchester Education Department when they say:

> Young people should develop the skills, attitudes, knowledge and values which enable them to take control of and responsibility for their own lives, fulfilling each individual's potential and ability to do so; to work together to bring about constructive and positive change and to achieve a more just world in which power and resources are more equally shared. This process should begin in the early years and continue throughout the entire educational experience (1991).

Other educationalists have offered similar conceptions of citizenship education, advocating a maximalist version. The work, for example, of Robin Richardson and the Runnymede Trust (1993) would seem to echo Manchester's views. There are also grounds for arguing that some of the ideas offered in the OFSTED discussion paper discussed in chapter 1 rest upon not too dissimilar a conception of the citizenship education.

National Curriculum Council: Curriculum Guidance 8 — Minimalist or maximalist?

The most significant national guidance to date has been NCC CG8. So where does it stand — what conception of citizenship education does it offer? The problem is that CG8 doesn't seem to offer a coherent model. CG8, like much NCC guidance in this area, is both minimalist and maximalist, and thus open to different and conflicting interpretations. On the one hand the definitions and aims of citizenship education would seem

91

Figure 1 KEY STAGE ACTIVITIES FROM CG8

KEY STAGE 3

Whole school activities

These might take the form of acting as a host group for visitors or assuming collective responsibility for an aspect of school or community life, eg keeping the school litter free, maintaining a display area, publishing a school/ community newsletter, voluntary work

KEY STAGE 4

Group and whole school activities

projects and placements within the community, eg painting and decorating, carrying out environmental improvements, gardening, work experience with young children, the elderly, the handicapped, the disabled and the disadvantaged.........community events, eg fun runs, community fairs, Junior Crime Prevention Panels

'voluntary organisations are important. Organisations such as St John's Ambulance, the Red Cross, Guides and Scouts promote caring responsible attitudes and enhance personal skills...'

---

to imply a narrow, minimalist version predominantly concerned with the provision of information. The aims of citizenship education are described in CG8 as:

> To establish the importance of positive, participative citizenship and provide the motivation to join in; to help pupils to acquire and understand essential information on which to base the development of their skills, values and attitudes towards citizenship.

At other times the document seems to offer something more in line with an empowerment model of citizenship education. For example, the descriptions of the sections on Pluralism and Citizen explicitly raise the need for education about inequalities and human rights. The section on Pluralism states:

This component helps pupils to appreciate that all citizens can and must be equal. It increases awareness of and works towards resolving some of the tensions and conflicts that occur between groups which perceive each other to be socially, racially, ethnically or culturally different. In this context it explores diversity, fairness and justice, co-operation and competition, prejudice and discrimination.

In the section on Being a Citizen we are told that:

Learning about duties, responsibilities and rights is central to this component. Rights include civil, political, social and human rights and how these might be violated by various forms of injustice, inequality and discrimination, including sexism and racism.

So there are clearly contradictory messages within the document with a maximalist position being articulated in some sections and a more minimalist view in others. However, the suggestions for key stages perhaps reveal where the document's heart lies. Fig 1 gives examples of suggested activities for key stages 3 and 4. A closer look at the suggestions reveals a very parochial view of citizenship, with the stress on doing good, wholesome and essentially non-challenging activities. Where is the critical edge, the challenge, the rigour we might expect?

What model of citizenship education are we concerned to promote?

We would place ourselves alongside those such as Manchester Education Department and the Runnymede Trust (1993) in wishing to develop a form of citizenship education which is maximalist. Education for citizenship should make a significant contribution to the development of the skills, understandings and attitudes outlined in chapter 1. As we have previously argued in *CG1* (1992) and *CG2* (1993), this education must, of necessity, embrace equal opportunities and multicultural policies and practices at every level. Such an education will also at its broadest encompass the terrains of the other cross-curricular themes, since we cannot conceive of producing effective, informed, critically aware future citizens who do not have an awareness and understanding of issues such as their own and others' health, of their impact on the non-human world, economic decision making and policy making.

93

Citizenship education and personal development

Citizenship education must be central to whole-school provision for personal development and to the fostering of the particular personal development outcomes outlined in Chapter 1. At one level these outcomes are themselves an attempt to spell out the kinds of citizens we hope to develop. So how can we provide planned opportunities for young people to develop these qualities? They will certainly need learning opportunities which give them first-hand experience of participation, equality, membership, freedoms, rights, responsibilities through schools councils, through extracurricular activities, through teaching and learning styles which encourage participation, control, autonomy and collaboration. They need opportunities to explore and question important issues which confront them now and in the future — such issues will range from the highly personal to the global. They need to develop a range of skills, personal and social. They will need to experience equality of opportunity and to develop a positive and informed awareness of inequalities and how to combat them. This requires them to have opportunities to explore areas of their lives and those of others in a critical, questioning manner, areas which cut across the heart of democratic living and citizenship.

In *Curriculum Guidance No 1* (1992) we tried to outline some of these areas and issues through a framework for delivering personal development through the cross-curricular elements. We now return to this framework to see how it might help us to plan a broad, maximalist model of citizenship education.

The case studies: *Ourselves* and *Food and Sustainability*

The two case studies which follow attempt to provide some ideas on planning for education for citizenship within the *taught curriculum* — alongside of the wider curriculum. Attention will need to be given to school aims and ethos and the ways in which these are reflected and affirmed through assemblies; whole school policies on, for example, equal opportunities, teaching and learning, behaviour and bullying; democratic structures of consultation and decision making. Indeed a maximalist approach would require attention to all these aspects of the institution.

Case study one: Ourselves KS1/2

Setting the curriculum context

Ourselves is a familiar and popular KS1 or 2 topic, it is successfully used to deliver a range of curriculum areas and an obvious vehicle for promoting pupils' personal development. Yet typical planning for the topic often excludes explicit references to provision for so doing. Typical topic webs for *Ourselves,* seem to miss out crucial stages of thinking, to do with the identification of some personal development outcomes from the topic; and of the key issues and areas of exploration about ourselves with which we would want to engage pupils.

Ourselves and citizenship education

The topic has the potential to enable pupils to explore aspects of all the cross-curricular themes: pupils can better understand their health, their relationship to the physical environment, their future roles as consumers, employers and employees. However, whilst all the themes may be touched upon it is helpful to isolate which would be at the heart of the topic. For us the theme which underpins all exploration of ourselves is citizenship, as it is citizenship education which makes explicit a central concern: the relationship between the individual and society.

Ourselves and personal development outcomes

The topic of ourselves provides opportunities for pupils to develop a range of skills, knowledge and attitudes. We would envisage using ourselves to promote, for example:

- high self-esteem
- self-awareness and self-knowledge
- confidence and assertiveness
- the ability to take responsibility for own actions and the effects of these on others
- understanding and sensitivity to the beliefs and ways of life of others
- the ability to maintain effective personal relationships within a moral framework
- a concern for justice and equality

However, such outcomes develop over time and the extent to which young children can be expected to demonstrate such outcomes will obviously vary. For example, while young children might be in the early stages of developing a sense of personal responsibility, they may well be capable of demonstrating a powerful concern for justice and equality. Given these complexities, teachers will nevertheless need to begin to identify some more precise learning outcomes for this age group and what might constitute realistic indicators of such development having taken place.

Using the framework to plan Ourselves

Having adopted the theme of citizenship as our central focus we then decided which of the central questions from the framework should underpin the topic. We selected three:

How do we acquire our social identities?

On what bases do people categorise others?

What is the nature of our rights and responsibilities in everyday life?

These questions were chosen because an exploration of ourselves is mainly concerned with the complex interrelationship between personal identity and culture and society. In particular:

'Who we are' is partially shaped by the culture(s) into which we are socialised and profoundly determined by factors such as our gender, 'race' and class as well as our genetic make-up.

How we see ourselves is influenced by others' perceptions of us. The ways we see others is influenced by a range of individual, social and cultural factors.

The particular interrelationship between our personal identity, culture and society can be fruitfully examined through both the rights we have as individuals and the responsibilities we have for others.

Using the organising questions

We use a number of the organising questions, as set out in Chapter, 1 linked to the three central questions. These help to frame the key questions in a number of specific ways:

(i) We use them as a kind of checklist to help us to ascertain which aspects of which cross-curricular themes we might be delivering through the topic. We can do this because the organising questions for each of the eleven questions range across the substance of the different themes.

(ii) We use them to help us to ensure that we are providing a range of different interpersonal, local, national and international contexts in which to explore the ideas.

(iii) We also use the questions to help us to ground some of the more abstract ideas within the central questions, to concretise them within people's personal experience.

The planning matrix

We are now at the stage where we can devise some key questions, key ideas, concepts, learning activities and assessment for ourselves. Fig 2 shows this planning matrix in detail and Fig 3 shows the planning cycle we use in constructing units of work and how this is applied to ourselves.

Figure 2: Matrix for Ourselves KS1/2

Key questions	concepts	key ideas	learning activities
What am I like?		our physical characteristics eg. body size and shape, hair, eyes, weight our personality our gender, 'race'	• interpreting photos of children in class at different ages • measuring and weighing • drawing each other • discussion work around 'what am I like? what is x like?'
How do I see myself?		our self-image and self-esteem eg. see ourselves as good or bad; kind or selfish; happy or sad; outgoing or shy.	• self-portraits, silhouettes, shadows • words, and pictures to describe ourselves • stories with focus on qualities of people (animals)
How have I learned to be like this?		socialisation through our families, culture, local neighbourhood inheriting of characteristics from our parents	• research into our families • photo exercise — who do I look like?

Figure 2: Matrix for Ourselves (continued)

Key questions	concepts	key ideas	learning activities
How do others see me?		How we appear to others is linked to things like our physical appearance, our behaviour, our body language, our speech others may make assumptions about us based on stereotypes	• words and pictures about people in class and around the school • interpreting photos — what can we tell about the person? • stories which challenge gender and stereotypes
How do other people's views of us affect how we see ourselves?		we may take on or reject others views of us accepting others' views can lead to false self-images whether we take on others' views of us can depend on our own self-esteem and confidence	• stories, discussion, how we can make others happy, sad etc and how others can make us happy etc • drawing faces of people sad, happy, frightened etc

Figure 2: Matrix for Ourselves (continued)

Key questions	concepts	key ideas	learning activities
How am I the same as others and how am I different?		We all share common human characteristics eg. we all experience fear, grief, happiness, anger, joy, sadness these experiences can be differently expressed due to things like our gender, culture etc. there are differences between people in terms of gender, culture, sexual orientation etc. differences can be used in ways which create inequalities	• project work to celebrate diversity in classroom • people in different countries

Figure 2: Matrix for Ourselves (continued)

Key questions	concepts	key ideas	learning activities
What responsibilities do others have towards me?		to provide physical and emotional care and support love and security	• work on being safe — road safety, talking to strangers, who looks after us • stories about being looked after and looking after others • art and design work redesigning playground, classroom to make it safe environment • code of practice in classroom
What responsibilities do I have towards others?		empathy sensitivity and understanding towards others treating others with fairness and equality	
What kinds of rights should I have?		the right to privacy and control my own body the right to be free from persecution, discrimination and any form of emotional and physical abuse right to health and security	

Figure 2: Matrix for Ourselves (continued)

Key questions	concepts	key ideas	learning activities
What kinds of beliefs do I have?		religious beliefs	• work on different cultures in school — cooking, making things, stories etc.
		moral beliefs about how we should act and treat others	
		cultural differences in our beliefs may be expressed through things like food we eat, how we dress, our social activities	
Where do my beliefs come from?		from our families	• tracing our families
		from our cultural backgrounds	• looking at our neighbourhood
		from where we live and the historical time in which we live	
Can I change how I am?		we can change through listening and learning from others; from new experiences and knowledge; through personal reflection and self-evaluation	• stories about people who change (become kinder, happier)
			• experiencing something new eg. visit, theatre group, film

Figure 3: planning cycle using the framework

1. Decide personal development outcomes to be fostered through the topic
2. Identify which themes best relate to the topic
3. Choose the most appropriate questions from the 11 central questions of the framework
4. Use the organising questions for these central questions to help frame some key questions for the topic
5. Identify appropriate key ideas, concepts, learning activities and assessment for the topic

Planning cycle for ourselves

1. **Personal development outcomes**

We would envisage using the topic to begin to promote the following outcomes

- high self-esteem
- self-awareness and self knowledge
- confidence and assertiveness
- responsibility for own actions and the effects of our actions on others
- understanding of and sensitivity towards beliefs and ways of life of others
- maintenance of interpersonal relationships within a moral framework
- concerned to promote justice and equality

2. **Themes** — we have decided to focus on citizenship as our lead theme for the topic

3. **Central questions**

- What is the nature of our rights and responsibilities in everyday life?
- On what bases do people categorise others?
- How do we acquire our social identities?

Figure 3: planning cycle using the framework (continued)

4. **Organising questions**

In what ways and why do things like our gender, religion, race etc influence who we are and how others see us?

How do we acquire our beliefs and values?

How and why do we sometimes change our beliefs and values during our lives?

In what ways are people similar?

In what ways are people different?

On what bases do we categorise other people and other social groups?

What effects do other peoples' views of us have on how we see and feel about ourselves?

What kinds of inequalities exist between people?

What kinds of rights should people have in relation to others?

What responsibilities do we have for others and for the no-human world?

How are our rights and responsibilities affected by such things as our age, gender, race, culture, status, material circumstances?

4. **Key questions for the topic** — for example:

    * What am I like?
    * How have I learned to be like I am?

5. **Concepts, key ideas, learning activities and assessment**

Case Study Two: Food and Sustainability At KS2

Setting the Curriculum Context

The study of food production and consumption has been a common one in both the primary and secondary curriculum and predates the introduction of the National Curriculum. Its links to education for citizenship have become more explicit as more teachers have sought to develop pupils' critical understanding of the relationship between the wealth of so-called first or northern world and third or southern world poverty. This study has encouraged a more conceptual approach through an analysis of such terms as 'interdependence' and 'sustainability'.

The development of the World Studies movement in primary and secondary education and the link between a more political/philosophical framework and classroom practice has been supported through materials such as *Teaching World Studies: An Introduction to Global Perspectives* (1982). The work of the development agencies, including Oxfam and the World Wildlife Found, although at times operating with competing agendas, have nevertheless supported teachers in clarifying a perspective on food production and consumption, within a more explicit study of economic and political structures and relationships.

Since the introduction of the National Curriculum, subjects such as technology, geography, history and science have been given potential legitimacy to explore topics around the theme of food. Closer inspection however reveals that their requirements have not necessarily enabled pupils at either Key Stage Two or Three to understand the interrelated factors which effect food and its production and consumption, analysed from the perspective of personal and cultural choice shaped by economic global decision making.

Curriculum space to explore these issues further in a crowded arena, has potentially been given by the cross-curricular themes. The documents produced by the NCC between 1989 and 1991 on Economic and Industrial Understanding, Citizenship, Environmental Education, and Health Education, make reference to aspects of food consumption and production. These documents, however, fail to speak to each other and provide the teacher and learner with little real sense of coherence when grappling with the complexities of a topic such as food. In this respect this example reflects the wider issue of the lack of a coherent framework in which the cross-curricular themes were designed. There is in addition no doubt that the pre-Dearing National Curriculum,with its heavy emphasis on content prescription and assessment, has restricted some of the previous classroom practice outlined above. In the new post-Dearing era, with the return, in part, of curriculum decision-making to schools, fresh opportunities may be afforded to teachers and pupils to reexamine such an important social and political topic as food. However without a clear framework opportunities to examine it in a systematic and rigorous manner may be restricted.

In wishing to link the topic of food to citizenship education we have sought to make an explicit link with the concept of sustainability. For this reason the unit outlined below has been underpinned by consideration of the following themes; those of Economic and Industrial Understanding (EIU), Citizenship and Environmental Education. In making explicit the concept of sustainability, we believe that pupils need to be encouraged to develop a critical view towards present economic arrangements and to begin to consider themselves as individuals within the social context of being global citizens. This approach seeks to stress that the impact of what we eat not only effects ourselves as individuals but has a direct impact on the lives of other citizens at a world level, as well as other species and the environment in general .

Food and Sustainability and Personal Development Outcomes

The topic of food provides opportunities to develop a range of under-standings, skills and attitudes. We would envisage using the topic specifically to promote:

> increased self-knowledge
> awareness of the need to take responsibility for one's own actions within a moral framework
> understanding of the beliefs, values and ways of life of others
> knowledge of the human physical world
> critical thinking; questioning the taken-for-granted
> promoting justice
> a concern for all forms of life.

As in the first case-study, these outcomes develop over time and the extent to which pupils will be able to demonstrate such outcomes will vary between individuals and groups. However, teachers will wish to gain confidence, making explicit the features or indicators they wish to promote in young children, and their visibility and consistency within different aspects of the curriculum.

Using the Framework to Plan Food and Sustainability

Having decided to use aspects of the three interrelated themes of Economic and Industrial Understanding, Citizenship and Environmental Education as a central focus we then, as in the example on food, select which of the central questions from the framework should underpin the topic. We again decided on three questions:

What is the nature of our rights and responsibilities in everyday life?

In what ways is the welfare of individuals and societies maintained?

What is our relationship to the non-human world?

Why these particular questions?

The three questions allow us to study the topic of food through examination of the interrelationship between our rights to consume and produce food of our choice within a 'free' society and yet to analyse these patterns in terms of our responsibilities as consumers, both to others in our own society and especially to those in the producing third world. The third question in particular, forces us to examine the impact of food production and consumption from a global perspective. This raises potentially difficult issues about the future development of the planet as a diverse ecosystem.

Using the Organising Questions

In planning this case study we also make use of a number of the organising questions linked with each central question. These are:

What responsibilities do we have for others and for the non-human world?

What responsibilities national and global organisations have for both people and the non-human world?

How are our rights and responsibilities influenced by religious belief and practice or by a moral code?

What do individuals need for their well-being?

What differences of welfare exists between individuals and groups?

What differences of welfare exists between nations? Why?

How should we respond to these differences?

What impact can human decisions and actions have upon the non-human world?

What responsibility do we have?

What responsibility do governments and non-government organisations have to the non-human world?

We use the organising questions, as we indicated in case study one, in a number of ways:

1. We use them as a kind checklist to help us to ascertain which aspects of specific cross curricular themes we might be delivering through the topic

2. We use them to help us to ensure that we are providing a range of different interpersonal, local, national and international contexts in which to explore the ideas .

3. We use the questions to help us ground some of the more abstract ideas within the central questions, to concretise them within people's personal experience.

In the case of 2 and 3 this process supports the writing of the key questions for the unit.

The Planning Matrix

We are now able to construct a planning matrix for food and sustainablity. The matrix is shown in fig.4 and the planning cycle is shown in fig.5.

This chapter has attempted to explore citizenship education as a critical strand of provision for pupils' personal development within schools. It has outlined how the framework we described in chapter 1 can be used to plan and implement citizenship education within the taught curriculum. However, as we made clear earlier, this taught provision will only be effective if it is part of a whole institutional approach in which all aspects of the school both reflect and contribute towards an explicit set of agreed aims which are concerned with the personal development of pupils.

Figure 4: MATRIX — FOOD AND SUSTAINABILITY KEY STAGE 2

Key questions	concepts	key ideas	learning activities
How do we decide what to eat?	culture wealth choice	personal preference awareness of health environmental awareness religious beliefs cultural practices wealth and income media influence	• interview work in classroom, school and local community • analysis of adverts • decision making exercises based on income, health requirements etc.
Where does our food come from?	interdependence	variety of food producers from local to global	• analysis of labels in shops and homes • location of these on world maps • interviews to determine peoples awareness of where food comes from
Why is food produced?	power	physical survival of human beings variety and choice for consumer markets and income for growers and producers	• case studies of companies producing particular food products eg. Cadburys, Unilever • Categorisation exerciser using evidence from different sources

Figure 4: MATRIX — FOOD AND SUSTAINABILITY KEY STAGE 2 (continued)

Key questions	concepts	key ideas	learning activities
Who produces the food?		the manufacturing, processing and distribution of food agriculture (subsistence and intensive) gender, age, class, geographical locationm and 'race' of producers	• case studies of range of food producers from local to global
How does what we eat affect others?	equality and inequality	growth and effects of fast food industry across societies economic, political and social effects of world markets on developing countries	• research activity based on case studies of fast food industries eg. MacDonalds
How does what we eat affect other species and the physical world?	sustainability	deforestation pressure on land effects on oceans and seas changing methods of animal rearing use of agro-chemicals	• group research tasks on different aspects eg. oceans and seas, land use, animal rearing, deforestation, hedgerows
Does everbody have enough to eat?	justice scarcity	differences of income between people, groups, societies notions of absolute and relative poverty in developed and developing countries	• analysis of range of evidence eg. statistical data, media, photographs, testimony drawn from range of societies

Figure 4: MATRIX — FOOD AND SUSTAINABILITY KEY STAGE 2 (continued)

Key questions	concepts	key ideas	learning activities
Why do some groups and societies have less to eat than others?	poverty	unequal trading relations between developing and developed countries population growth in poorer countries and communities poverty and unemplyment	• simulation games and role play exercises around trading
How can we sustain a better future for all?		more equal trading relations redistribution of wealth within and across societies more sustainable food production access to and control over technology	• presentations from groups arguing different positions • making of newspapers presenting different viewpoints

111

Figure 5: Planning cycle for food and sustainability

1. **Personal development outcomes**

We would envisage using the topic specifically to promote:

- increased self-knowledge
- awareness of the need to take responsibility for one's own actions within a moral framework
- understanding of the beliefs, values and ways of life of others
- Knowledge of the human physical world
- critical thinking; questioning the taken-for-granted
- promoting justice
- a concern for all forms of life

2. **Themes** — we decided on citizenship, environmental education and education for international understanding

3. **Central questions**

- What is the nature of our rights and responsibilities in every day life?
- In what ways is the welfare of individuals and societies maintained?
- What is our relationship to the non-human world?

4. **Organising questions**

What responsibilities do we have for others and for the non-human world?

What responsibilities do national and global organisations have for both people and the non-human world?

How are our rights and responsibilities influenced by religious belief and practice or by a moral code?

What do individuals need for their well-being?

What differences of welfare exist between individuals and groups?

What differences of welfare exist between nations? Why?

How should we respond to these differences?

Figure 5: Planning cycle for food and sustainability (continued)

What impact can human decisions and actions have upon the non-human world?

What responsibility do we have?

What responsibility do governments non-government organisations have to the non-human world?

5. **Key questions for the topic** — for example:

    *   How do we decide what to eat?

    *   Where does our food come from?

6. **Concepts, key ideas, learning activities and assessment**

References

Brown, C. (1991) Education for Citizenship: Old wine in new bottles?' *Citizenship* vol 1 and 2

Buck, M. and Inman, S. (1992) *Curriculum Guidance No 1: Whole School Provision for Personal and Social Development Centre for Cross- Curricular Initiatives*. Goldsmiths College

Commission on Citizenship Education (1990) Report. CCE

Development Education Centre (1987) *Food Matters*. Birmingham DEC

Hall, S. and Held, D. (1989) Citizens and Citizenship in (ed) Hall, S. and Jacques, M.: *New Times*. Lawrence and Wishart

Hicks, D. and Townley, C. (eds) (1982) *Teaching World Studies: An Introduction to a Global Perspective*. Longman

Hurd, D. quoted by S. Cook in the *Guardian*, 9th November 1988

Mc Goughlin, T. (1992) Citizenship, Diversity and Education: a philosophical perspective. *Journal of Moral Education*, Vol 21 No 3

Manchester City Education Department (1991) *Implementing the Whole Curriculum*. Manchester

National Commission on Education (1993) *Learning to Succeed.*

National Curriculum Council: Circular No 6 (1990) *The National Curriculum and the Whole Curriculum*, NCC

National Curriculum Council (date?) *Curriculum Guidance No 8: Education for Citizenship*, NCC

Runneymede Trust (19993) *Equality Assurance in Schools*. Trentham Books

Chapter 6

Reading, Identity and Personal Development

Elizabeth Plackett

> Everyone knows that to be at home in a literate society is a feeling as well as a fact. (Margaret Meek, 1991)

In the late 70s, after *The Bullock Report* had recommended that each school should have an organised policy for language across the curriculum, establishing every teacher's involvement in language and reading development throughout the years of schooling' (DES, 1975), many local education authorities required all their secondary schools to produce a policy to show how they would develop language across the curriculum. Although many policy documents found their way into filing cabinets, not many actually ensured that children's reading, writing and spoken language were systematically developed in all subjects, rather than being seen as merely an English department responsibility.

Now, however, what failed in the liberal 70s may have a better chance of success in the more directive 90s. The new National Curriculum orders include a statement for all subjects (with the exception of English, Welsh and Modern Languages, whose orders are of course entirely concerned with language) which lays out clearly that all teachers have a responsibility for developing children's language. The Ofsted *Framework*

115

for the Inspection of Schools also requires inspectors to evaluate pupils' 'competence in the key skills within reading, writing, speaking and listening ... in the curriculum as a whole' (Ofsted, 1994). It looks, therefore, as if, ironically, nearly twenty years later, language across the curriculum may at last be taken seriously.

This chapter considers the question of a whole school policy for reading. A policy on reading forms only part of a policy for language across the curriculum, and reading development would need to be considered alongside the development of writing and talk. However, by taking reading as a case-study of a cross-curricular skill, I hope to look in more detail at the practical implications of a whole school approach. In reality, of course, reading cannot be arbitrarily split off from the other language modes. I begin by considering why, legal constraints apart, we need a whole school approach to developing reading in the secondary school; go on to argue that developing as a fluent and competent reader is a personal rather than a mechanical process; and finally make some suggestions about how a school could begin to put a whole school reading policy into effect.

Why a reading policy?

It is perhaps not surprising that most primary schools have cross-curricular policy statements for reading whereas in the secondary school these tend to be 'English department documents rather than cross-curricular policies for the whole school' (DES, 1989). In the primary school, the class teacher is responsible for all the learning of her class and is likely to see all subject areas as providing opportunities for reading development. In the secondary school, on the other hand, subject boundaries tend to be sharply delineated and fairly inflexible. While teaching in some subjects may include the teaching of some aspects of reading — reading maps, reading historical sources, reading charts or databases — reading development as a whole is often seen as the responsibility of the English department.

Nevertheless, despite the fact that there are understandable reasons why secondary schools may find it difficult to develop effective cross-curricular reading policies, a whole school approach is necessary. Without it, it will be difficult to raise standards of reading and with them standards of learning generally. This is not to imply that standards of reading have fallen, since there is actually evidence that they have risen (Gorman et al, 1991). What has happened, of course, is that expectations have risen. The range and difficulty of the reading that we now expect the majority of pupils to be able to cope with by the time they leave school were, not so long ago, only expected of a minority. Not only do we now expect of the majority forms of literacy which were once the preserve of an elite, but the nature of literacy itself has changed and will continue to change. Reading now no longer merely means reading books or even reading print: we now expect pupils to read using the new technologies and to 'read' media texts.

The 'information explosion' will place a far greater emphasis on being able to select and evaluate information rather than merely retrieving it. If pupils are to meet these challenges there will need to be a coherent approach to reading across the curriculum rather than the somewhat random one which exists at present. Where there is no common agreement about reading, pupils are likely to find that they meet widely different expectations of and approaches to reading as they move from subject to subject. This will make it impossible to ensure that the reading curriculum as a whole provides opportunities for pupils to develop the full range of skills and it will also make it difficult to ensure progression from key stage 2 to key stage 3 and throughout the secondary school.

Reading Skills

In an interesting discussion of different approaches to the teaching of reading, Elaine Millard comments that

> there is an antithesis governing discussions about all aspects of reading... which sets, at one polarity, a series of hierarchically struc- tured language skills, directed to functional purposes that can be practised through repetitive tasks and finally 'mastered', and at the other a model of growth through the imaginative familiarity with stories, songs and traditional rhymes, where development is seen as a continuous process (Millard, 1994).

I see a similar dichotomy at work in the secondary school where, on the one hand, English teachers are expected to take on the 'personal' side of reading, to help pupils to develop emotionally and imaginatively through the texts which they read, whereas reading done elsewhere in the curriculum is often seen as 'functional' and therefore impersonal and neutral. I would like to offer an alternative view: that reading is never a neutral skill but one whose acquisition is closely associated with a sense of one's personal identity. I would also like to challenge the idea that reading skills can be hierarchically ordered into 'basic' and 'higher-order' skills and to argue that all stages of reading involve active, critical, meaning-making processes.

Reading and identity

Although the word 'skill' suggests something impersonal and value-free which can be mechanically acquired, I believe it would be mistaken to regard the skills of reading in this way. There is considerable evidence to show that a child's development as a reader is influenced by his or her sense of personal and cultural identity and that children develop as readers in ways that seem to them to fit with their sense of identity. I would like to take the case of gender and reading as an example of the way in which reading and identity are interwoven. For decades we have known that there are very significant differences between boys and girls in relation to reading. We know that girls and boys have different tastes in reading: girls tend to prefer fiction while boys prefer non-fiction. At the same time, girls read more than boys. Both these findings are replicated among the adult population. Thirdly, girls achieve more highly than boys in reading. This is true at all ages from key stage 1 SAT's to A level English. In the past this was considered so 'normal' that the scoring of reading tests (and of the 11+ exam) was often statistically adjusted so as to remove the imbalance.

The nature of these differences between boys and girls in their reading suggests that they are cultural and not innate, as has sometimes been argued in the past. Rather, it seems that, from a very early age, both boys and girls are aware of what reading 'means' in our culture. They observe that being a keen reader of fiction seems a more 'feminine' activity; whereas preferring facts is apparently more 'masculine'. Children are learning to read at an age when they are very conscious of adopting 'gender-appropriate' behaviour and they incorporate into this their view of the kind of reader they are. Role models may play an important part here. Girls will see many women reading (including their teacher, since most infant teachers are women). It may be harder for boys to find role models, especially if the adult males they know do not read. Where they do find a role model, the effect may be very significant. In her case study of the reading of three boys, Hilary Minns shows how influential is the role of their fathers: 'The boys, consciously or otherwise, model some of their own reading behaviour on their fathers' particular reading styles and preferences.' (Minns, 1993). If boys are not presented with evidence that it is possible both to be male and to enjoy reading, they may unconsciously choose to preserve their sense of their masculinity at the expense of their literacy.

It appears then that, as children are learning to read, they are also learning how reading relates to their gender identity. How reading is understood and interpreted is at least partly dependent on what they already know about their gender identity (though of course there are wide individual differences too). The implication for the teacher is, therefore, that reading cannot be seen as a neutral or merely mechanical skill but is one which comes already laden with values and interpretations. If the teacher does not deal with this fact — or worse, if she merely confirms the pupils' assumptions offering *Sweet Valley High* books to the girls, *The Guiness Book of Records* to the boys — she will not be helping pupils to explore a broader, less stereotyped gender-identity.

She may also not be helping pupils to develop the full range of reading skills. It may be that one reason why boys lack fluency in reading is because they have not had the very extensive experience of sustained, continuous reading which a preference for fiction has provided for many girls. Nor, often, have boys developed the ability (or desire) to empathise with others, to experience what life feels like from another's point of view, which many girls have developed through their identification with characters in stories. On the other hand, girls, who have often been assumed to be the successful ones in reading, may also not have developed certain skills. Boys' reading of non-fiction may help them to develop skills such as skimming and scanning, identifying interesting pieces of information, reading charts and graphs and so on. Girls' relative lack of experience in this area may mean that they are not developing these skills, which they will need to use in their reading in a range of subject areas. In other words, girls' success in English may be at the expense of their success in other subject areas — ones which are perhaps more likely to lead to achievement in adult life.

What appears at first sight, therefore, to be a simple matter of personal choice, may result in disadvantage for both girls and boys if a *laissez-faire* approach is adopted. This emphasises that 'equality is not merely a matter of 'offering' opportunities: rather, it is a a matter of taking positive action to ensure that opportunities are taken up' (Runnymede Trust, 1993), in this case by a structured approach which allows all pupils to experience and enjoy a wide range of texts.

I have spent some time looking at the relationship between reading and gender in order to demonstrate that the way in which children acquire a 'basic skill' is not in fact a neutral process but is strongly influenced by the child's sense of personal identity, of who they are as a person and as a learner. This is just one example; there is evidence to show that reading development is also influenced by 'race' and by class, and no doubt by other factors too. We need to take this into account, rather than assuming that reading is a mechanical, impersonal skill, so that we can ensure that all pupils experience and enjoy a range of texts, and learn the skills needed to read (and write) those texts.

A hierarchy of skills?

There is a common assumption that reading development is hierarchical in nature: it begins with the 'basic' skills of reading — learning to decode words — then, perhaps, the pupil moves on to 'higher-order' skills which involve reflecting on what is read, and acquiring research and study skills. The Dearing Report endorses this view of reading development: it recommends an emphasis on 'basic skills' at key stage 1; in the first two years of key stage 2 there should be a 'development and consolidation of the basic skills of ... literacy' while in the remaining two years of key stage 2 there should be 'a consolidation of basic skills and development of higher-order skills' (Dearing, 1994).

Such a concept of reading development fits conveniently with a curriculum organised on a linear and hierarchical basis, but it does not match what we know about how children's reading actually develops. Many very young children, who are not yet able to 'decode' text unaided, demonstrate 'higher-order' skills in their reading; they are able to read between the lines, make comparisons between texts, make judgements on books. Indeed, the astonishingly rich and subtle picture book literature which is available for young children often actually requires such skills for its enjoyment. 'Higher-order' skills, then, are not 'higher' in the sense that they are necessarily later acquired, though we might reasonably argue that they are 'higher' in terms of the value which we might put on them.

The notion of a hierarchy of reading skills has also been challenged by research which attempted to find out whether it was possible to separate 'lower-level' comprehension skills, such as understanding the meaning of individual words, from 'higher- level' skills such as understanding the overall ideas of the passage or forming judgements of those ideas. The researchers assessed children's performance on these different 'sub-skills' but were unable to show that such distinctions existed; rather, where there were differences in children's ability to comprehend what they read, it was an overall difference in the 'ability and willingness to reflect' on what was read (Lunzer and Gardner, 1979). The implication therefore is that reading is a unitary, single skill rather than a hierarchy of sub-skills. If that is so, the 'ability and willingness to reflect' should be encouraged and developed from the beginning, rather than being considered to be a 'higher-order' skill to be added on once the basic skills have been acquired.

Development in reading will not, therefore, consist in progressing up a ladder of ever more difficult skills but in learning to reflect on an increasingly wide range and variety of texts. In this sense reading development is spiral rather than linear; pupils will be practising and extending their skills in new contexts rather than learning completely new skills. The implication is not, however, that such development will automatically happen through exposure to the reading demands of the curriculum — pupils will need support for their development, and they will need a reading curriculum which allows for continuity and progression in that development.

What kind of policy?

I have been arguing that reading (of all kinds) is closely related to a child's sense of his or her own personal identity. This is reflected in the choices which children make about their reading, in the skills which they develop and, indeed, whether they choose to read voluntarily at all. To contribute to pupils' reading development, a reading policy would need to help them to sustain and extend their sense of who they are. One familiar aspect of this is by examining the range of texts across the curriculum and ensuring that a diverse range of people are represented and that stereotypes are not perpetuated. Perhaps less familiar is the need to ensure that pupils' own sense of their personal identity does not cut them off from the full range of reading experiences as, for example, may happen to girls if they choose to read only narrative.

I have also been proposing a particular view of reading development, one in which pupils can be critical and reflective readers at all stages. A reading policy therefore needs to ensure that pupils' reading is being developed in ways which promote engaged and committed learning rather than learning by rote or the mechanical completion of reading tasks. For example, reference or library skills need to be taught in such a way that pupils are able to use them in real research or investigative tasks rather than merely able to demonstrate competence in decontextualised exercises. A policy which allows for progression in reading will ensure that pupils meet an increasingly wide and complex variety of texts rather than that they move from 'basic' to 'higher-order' skills.

In the remainder of this chapter I outline some of the ways in which a school can begin to develop a coherent and effective approach to reading. Three main areas are examined: encouraging independent reading; developing the reading curriculum; and providing for inexperienced readers.

Independent reading

Most schools are likely to want to encourage all pupils to develop the habit of reading for pleasure and to come to see themselves as readers with preferences and tastes which they can articulate and pursue independently. As well as the obvious advantage of the potential pleasure which can be gained from reading, it is also a means to explore the world beyond yourself, to enter alternative worlds and to explore other points of view, whether through fictional or factual texts. It offers the opportunity for pupils both to find their own experiences mirrored in books and to discover alternative ways of being; to extend, as well as confirm their sense of identity.

Those who are enthusiastic readers are also likely to be developing and improving their reading because they are giving themselves the necessary practice. In other words, encouraging independent reading is an important strategy for raising reading standards — and therefore for raising standards in many areas of the curriculum. Nevertheless, the advantages and pleasures of reading are not obvious to all pupils — the older pupils get, the less they tend to read — and there is a particular falling off in the first years of the secondary school. This is not an immutable trend, however; schools can certainly make a significant difference to the numbers of pupils who become and remain keen readers (Ingham, 1981, West, 1986).

Schools which make most difference are likely to see promoting reading as a whole school responsibility, not merely the province of the English department. Indeed, many of the most effective ways of encouraging reading require a whole school commitment to provide resources and time for a variety of activities. Such a commitment also indicates to pupils, parents (and teachers) that reading is a highly valued and high status activity.

A number of strategies for encouraging reading involve parents or other adults in reading with children. These seem to be successful because they provide one-to-one attention from an adult interested in the child's reading and perhaps also because they provide a role model of an adult who enjoys reading. One scheme, adopted from the primary school, is PACT (Parents and Children and Teachers), a home/school reading scheme which involves parents agreeing to share books regularly with their child. A record card is commonly used for parents and teachers to exchange comments on the child's reading. PACT has the great advantage of involving parents in their children's learning and of enabling a dialogue between parent and teacher about the child's development as a reader. By continuing a practice from the primary school, PACT schemes encourage children to maintain their reading into Year 7 — a time when it often begins to decline.

There are a number of other strategies which involve parents or other adults in supporting pupils' reading. Family Literacy Groups provide opportunities for parents and their children to come to after-school or Saturday classes and work together on reading and writing activities. This can often be a way of helping adults to develop their own literacy, as well as providing ways for them to help their children. Other strategies for involving adults in 'sharing' reading with pupils include visiting adults from the local area who are willing to work with pupils on a regular basis; teacher 'mentors' who make time to read with pupils, perhaps during lunch-time or at after-school reading clubs; student teachers on teaching practice or university undergraduates acting as volunteers for Community Service Volunteers (who have a scheme specifically for voluntary work in school). Not only adults, but pupils themselves, can contribute, either as sixth-formers working with younger pupils or even for paired reading within the same class. The experience of being a role model for younger pupils can also be a very beneficial one, involving secondary pupils in cross-phase projects, reading or writing with primary school pupils.

The profile of reading in the school can also be raised by setting up school bookshops or book clubs where pupils have the opportunity of becoming book-owners, something which is often important to pupils' sense of themselves as readers. Book events of various kinds, such as visits from authors, sponsored reading for charity or book weeks, all indicate that reading is an important and enjoyable activity. Time can also be made for reading through lunch-time or after-school reading clubs or through a timetabled whole-school reading period several times a week.

The school library has a vital part to play in promoting reading in the school. The library can be a dynamic place which ensures that pupils encounter a wide range of interesting books which can extend and develop their reading preferences. Regularly changing displays can represent many different cultures, different genres of books, and a wide range of authors. The librarian can also play an active role in many of the other activities described above.

Obviously the English department also has a major role to play in promoting reading; English teachers are likely to have the best opportunity to discuss books with individual children and to use their specialist knowledge of books and reading to recommend books which will enthuse a reluctant reader or extend the range of one who has stuck in a rut. Nevertheless, promoting reading should not be solely the responsibility of the English teacher or the librarian. A whole-school approach to encouraging reading tells pupils that reading is valued by all teachers and is, indeed, more likely to 'make a difference' than an approach associated only with one department.

The reading curriculum

The reading curriculum is simply the sum total of all the reading carried out across all subjects. Describing it as a curriculum emphasises the need to ensure that pupils have a coherent experience of reading across the curriculum, that the demands on their reading skills from subject to subject are consistent and appropriate, and that there is continuity and progression from year to year. This means that all teachers need to see themselves as responsible for developing reading skills and for teaching pupils to cope with the kinds of reading which are specific to their subject.

Monitoring reading

A major investigation into the use of reading in the secondary curriculum (Lunzer and Gardner, 1979) revealed that a surprisingly brief share of pupils' time in lessons was spent reading. Often this reading was in tiny bursts of less than a minute at a time. This strange phenomenon was produced by pupils spending a good deal of time copying from books or from the board, or scanning their textbooks in search of answers to questions. If this pattern remains the same (and it may be that reading has been marginalised even further in order to provide 'access' to the curriculum) then pupils will not be getting the practice they need to improve their reading. Indeed, teachers often unwittingly help pupils to evade reading by paraphrasing texts for them, thus enabling them to complete the task without any further reading.

The same research found that many pupils were being asked to read texts that were simply too difficult for them. There is also evidence to show that many pupils who have no problems reading and understanding stories do have difficulty with the specialist styles of writing that they encounter in their textbooks (Perera, 1986, Littlefair, 1991). For many Year 7 pupils, secondary subject textbooks pose different reading demands from the books which they have met in the primary school. For example, the information books which they may have used for topic work in the primary school are structured differently from secondary textbooks. These commonly have complex lay-outs and require a different way of working, requiring pupils to use several different kinds of information on the page in order to carry out the tasks set.

It is important that all departments monitor the amount and level of reading that pupils are expected to do. A relatively easy way of doing this across departments is to record all the reading done by one class across a particular period of time, say one week. Although this is only a rough guide, it can reveal inconsistencies and gaps and can give an indication of how well the reading curriculum is likely to support pupils' reading development. Individual departments can then review the amount and difficulty of reading in their own lessons and consider whether any action needs to be taken.

Developing reading skills

Among the skills which pupils need to develop are the ability to vary their reading style according to the nature of the text and of the tasks; being able for example to skim for the overall gist or scan for specific pieces of information; the ability to read reflectively and critically; and the ability to find out effectively from books and other sources of information. As I argued earlier, teaching such skills through decontextualised exercises does not automatically mean that the skills can be transferred to a 'real' task. It is more effective if a reading curriculum is constructed which provides real opportunities for learning and practising these skills.

Most teachers want to use reading to help pupils to understand new concepts and ideas. Unfortunately, the kinds of traditional comprehension questions which sometimes follow reading rarely encourage pupils to really engage with the new ideas, and often pupils can answer the questions without any real thought at all. Collaborative work, and tasks which set pupils problems to solve through reading, rather than individual question- answering, are more likely to result in work which genuinely involves thought rather than merely information retrieval.

Teachers often expect pupils to be competent 'researchers', able to locate and record information and integrate it into their own work without wholesale copying. These are difficult skills and perhaps the expectations are sometimes unrealistic. Separate information skills courses can be useful but unless opportunities to practise these skills are built into work across the curriculum they are unlikely to become real to pupils. Schools need to identify which skills they expect pupils to be able to use at different stages of their school career and then to plan them into specific units of work across the curriculum. The skills should be not just the information-locating ones of using catalogues, databases, contents pages and so on but the more difficult ones of planning, setting questions to be answered, selecting and rejecting information, and presenting findings. All these skills need to be practised from the start but the scale of the investigation and the extent and nature of the sources can become more complex and difficult as pupils progress up the school.

Subject-specific reading

So far I have been discussing the ways in which all teachers can help pupils to develop a broad range of reading skills. However, there will be some kinds of reading which are specific to particular subjects. I mentioned earlier the demands which secondary textbooks will make of Year 7 pupils. Individual subject textbooks will be organised in different ways, have different kinds of lay-outs using colour-coding, bold or italic type to indicate different sections and so on, and pupils will need to be helped to 'read' the significance of these features.

There will be specific language differences too. Most teachers are used to introducing new vocabulary to pupils but most subjects will also use styles and forms of language which pupils may not have encountered before, especially if their main reading has been narrative. Examples are the use of the passive in science and sometimes in other subjects; new genres such as the design brief and evaluation in Design Technology; reports, descriptions, accounts of processes, discussions of points of view, and so on in several subjects.

Pupils need to become familiar with the structures of these genres; one of the most useful ways in which this can happen is when they hear texts read aloud. In this way they become familiar with the new language and will find it more predictable when they come to read it on their own. Equally importantly, they will have a better idea what is expected when they are asked to write in these forms themselves. Sometimes it may help to focus directly on the language used, for example, by underlining the words and phrases used when presenting an argument ('on the one hand', 'on the other hand', 'however', etc) and then trying these out themselves. This is more likely to be effective than the more abstract advice sometimes given ('try and give both points of views'). Other kinds of 'reading' which occur in many texts across the curriculum include reading maps, tables, graphs, diagrams, charts, and so on and pupils will often need specific help in reading these when they occur.

Inexperienced readers

The third strand of a reading policy concerns the provision for pupils with reading difficulties. Many inexperienced readers have become demoralised by an increasing sense of failure and may never have learnt that reading can be anything other than a chore, to be avoided whenever possible. For them, the discovery that reading can be enjoyable is crucial, and many of the strategies for promoting reading for pleasure are of direct relevance to inexperienced readers. Since the majority of poor readers are usually boys, it is important that they have opportunities to find role-models of male readers among the adults who support them, and that they can find books to read which they see as appropriate to their gender. By this I don't mean that teachers should confirm stereotyped choices but that they should build on pupils' preferences in moving them on to a wider range of texts, for example, by encouraging boys to read narrative by providing stories which use comic or cartoon formats as well as more traditional types of fiction.

Ways of providing help for pupils with reading difficulties have changed considerably over the last decade, from provision largely focused on specific help with reading out of the mainstream classroom, to provision largely focused on access to the mainstream curriculum. *The new Code of Practice on the Identification and Assessment of Special Educational Needs* has a greater emphasis on precise assessment of individual needs than much recent advice, and this may well highlight the fact that a large number of pupils with special needs of all kinds have problems with literacy. This may lead to a greater emphasis on support for individual reading development. However, many pupils will need both support with the reading of the curriculum and specific help in improving their literacy.

Access to the curriculum for inexperienced readers is sometimes interpreted as entailing a form of differentiation which provides simplified (or in extreme cases, reading-free) materials for those pupils. Sometimes the level of difficulty of reading is too high for a large number of the pupils, and then it would be appropriate to rewrite materials for the whole class. However, simplifying all work for individual pupils is not usually either practical or desirable. It is very time-consuming and actually quite difficult to do effectively. (A well-simplified text will often be longer than the original.) It also fails to create a situation in which pupils can develop 'higher-order' reading skills. All too often, pupils using simplified materials are occupied in mechanical busy-work and get into a vicious spiral of low expectations and lack of involvement in the work, leading to low achievement and even lower expectations. On the other hand, if the classroom is organised so that pupils can participate in the kind of collaborative, active reading described in the previous section, inexperienced readers will be able to take part in tasks which they could not manage on their own. Hearing the text read aloud by the teacher or by one of the group, means that they will not have to struggle with the actual decoding of the text but will have access to its meaning.

It may be that providing real access to the curriculum helps pupils to become more motivated to learn and that they are then able to improve their reading through the reading curriculum which they experience. However, there are likely to be some pupils whose difficulties are less easily resolved and who will need specific help with reading. It can be tempting at this stage to take a 'back-to-basics' approach and adopt a programme which attempts to drill pupils in what are considered 'basic skills'. I have argued earlier against a separation of 'basic' and 'higher-order' skills; it is important for these pupils that reading is taught in such a way that they begin to develop their own purposes for reading and recover a sense of what reading has to offer. Methods of teaching reading which emphasise the decoding of individual words at the expense of the purposeful and enjoyable getting of meaning from texts, are in danger of producing readers who see reading as a mechanical process which does not require involvement or critical thought on their part. Such readers are unlikely to sustain their progress once the programme has been completed. Nor are they likely to develop a long-term view of reading as an enjoyable and purposeful part of their lives.

I have been arguing in this chapter for a view of reading which is not mechanical or impersonal, but which requires critical thinking at all levels and is closely related to one's sense of personal identity. There are those who do not share this view but look back instead to a golden age when formal, 'rigorous' methods of teaching ensured a more literate population. Such a golden age, of course, never existed; indeed, it seems that in every age there is nostalgia for an earlier, imagined educational past. But it is useful to remember that the methods to which we are now being urged to return arose from a social context in which rote learning, recitation from the Bible and accurate copying in copperplate handwriting were required skills for obedient workers and for the clerks of an age without CD-ROMs, word-processors or photocopiers, let alone the 'information super-highway'.

We, however, are preparing pupils for the reading of the twenty-first century and they will need very different skills. Already employers are telling us that the ability to decode and follow written instructions correctly is far from enough — our pupils will need to be critical, versatile and independent readers. For these qualities to develop, all teachers need to find ways of presenting reading as something which is personally significant to pupils and which is learnt through active, meaningful tasks. By doing this they will be not only preparing pupils for their future working lives but also empowering them to develop as thoughtful, reflective readers and to use their reading to extend their sense of the kind of person they can be.

References

Dearing, R. (1994) *The National Curriculum and its Assessment: final report* (the Dearing Report), SCAA

Department of Education and Science (1975) *A Language for Life* (The Bullock Report), HMSO

Department of Education and Science (1989) *Reading Policy and Practice at Ages 5-14*, DES

Gorman, T. et al (1989) *Language for Learning: A Summary Report on the 1988 APU Surveys of Language Performance*, SEAC

Ingham, J. (1981) *Books and Reading Development: The Bradford Book Flood Experiment*, Heinemann

Littlefair, A. (1991) *Reading All Types of Writing: The Importance of Genre and Register for Reading Development*, Open University

Lunzer, E. and Gardner, K. (eds) (1979) *The Effective Use of Reading*, Heinemann

Meek, M. (1991) *On Being Literate*, Bodley Head

Millard, E. (1994) *Developing Readers in the Middle Years*, Open University

Minns, H. (1993) 'Three Ten Year Old Boys and their Reading' in Barrs, M. and Pidgeon, S. (eds) *Reading the Difference: Gender and Reading in the Primary School*, CLPE

Office for Standards in Education (1994) *Handbook for the Inspection of Schools*, Ofsted

Perera, K. (1986) 'Some Linguistic Difficulties in School Textbooks' in Gilham, B. (ed) *The Language of School Subjects*, Heinemann

Runnymede Trust (1993) *Equality Assurance in Schools: Quality, Identity, Society*, Trentham Books/Runnymede Trust

West, A. (1986) 'The Production of Readers', *English Magazine* 17

Chapter 7

Making sense of the spiritual and moral

Lynne Broadbent

Setting the Context

The year 1988 proved a landmark in the development of education practice. This was the the year of Education Reform Act which instituted the National Curriculum, which defined core and foundation subjects, which specified the knowledge, skills and understanding that pupils are expected to have at the end of each key stage, which talked of programmes of study and set up processes for assessment. It was an Act which has drawn controversy and criticism ever since.

However, it was this same Act, indeed, the same section of the 1988 Act, which identified provision for the National Curriculum, which spoke also of the need of the curriculum to consider the personal development of pupils.

Chapter 40 of the Education Reform Act, entitled 'The Curriculum', opened with these now well-known words:

> The curriculum for a maintained school satisfies the requirements ...
> if it is a balanced and broadly based curriculum which —

(a) promotes the spiritual, moral, cultural, mental and physical development of pupils and of society; and

(b) prepares such pupils for the opportunities, responsibilities and experiences of adult life.

These statements raise a number of issues. Firstly, they suggest that the curriculum is not solely about the development of knowledge and skills, but also about the development of the whole person, and that the 'spiritual' and 'moral' are both aspects of this development. The inclusion of these statements would seem also to acknowledge that the development of the whole person will not automatically follow from adherence to attainment targets and programmes of study, but will require close attention from those involved in planning the curriculum. Furthermore, it is anticipated that provision for this development will affect pupils not only during their time in school, but will continue to affect their opportunities and experiences in adult life. Here then would seem to be a clear statement of the values held by the legislators of the Act: that a concern for personal development, for the education of the whole child in the primary school, the whole pupil in the secondary school and the developing adult, should lie at the heart of the educational process. Whether these values have permeated curriculum planning, or indeed, whether it was ever possible for these values to permeate the structures of the National Curriculum, is a matter for debate.

References to spiritual and moral development were certainly not new — the terms had appeared in the 1944 Education Act which made it incumbent upon every local authority to: 'contribute towards the spiritual, moral, mental and physical development of the community' and had been explored in various educational documents in the interim (see, for example, DES, 1977). However, in 1988, spiritual and moral development in the curriculum became essential to the fulfilling of the Act and, after the 1992 Education Act, have become subject to Inspection under the OFSTED Framework (1993). Under the Framework, spiritual and moral development, alongside social and cultural development, account for one of the four concerns to be inspected in a school — a substantial part of the inspection process. Furthermore, as we shall see, responsibility for this lies with us all, whether we are classroom teachers, curriculum specialists or part of the school management. It becomes a matter of urgency, then, to think about what we mean by spiritual and moral development, where we might find it within the curriculum and how it might be inspected.

Breaking down barriers

There are often barriers to discussion of the above issues. The first is confusion about the term 'spiritual'. Popular thought locates it solely within the 'religious', rendering it of little interest or positively unacceptable to many who feel no affinity with organised religion. Even a cursory glance at the National Curriculum Council's Discussion Paper, *Spiritual and Moral Development* (1993) reassures us that this is not the intention and such a narrow understanding of spiritual development would 'exclude from its scope the majority of pupils in our schools who do not come from overtly religious backgrounds'. The document clearly states that the term should be seen as ' applying to something fundamental in the human condition'.

The second barrier concerns the frequent conflation of spiritual and moral development in statements by government ministers and in the popular press. This inhibits clear definition and understanding of the role of education in the development of both. There may well be some overlap in spiritual and moral development if we promote moral education in one particular sense. If, for example, we encourage pupils to engage with human issues which may be controversial, such as the taking of life, say, or community responsibility, if we explore different beliefs and foster the development of empathy with conflicting viewpoints, encourage experiences in decision-making and opportunities to reflect upon the possible outcomes of those decisions, then there is considerable overlap. Both spiritual and moral development relate, in part, to questions about 'personhood' and individual and collective human experience. However, too frequently the press and even some current educational documents restrict their descriptions of moral education to the need to conform to given social standards of behaviour rather than to the development of knowledge and understanding and the skills of informed decision-making. (It is crucial to note here that for most religious adherents, the spiritual and moral areas of experience will undoubtedly be meshed, both emanating from a single source of authority, and that any attempt to separate the two would conflict with the individual's holistic experience of life.)

The third possible barrier to exploring spiritual and moral development relates to a concern that it might involve importing something new into the curriculum and may involve us in a different kind of relationship with our pupils. We may fear overloading the curriculum or fear that any relationship which places us in the role of priest or moral arbiter would lie uncomfortably with our current practice. The OFSTED Discussion Paper of 1994 on *Spiritual, Moral, Social and Cultural Development*, reassures us here on both accounts. It identifies two strands in looking at spiritual and moral development, namely the curriculum and the personal relationships in the school. The Paper seeks 'to draw out the potential within the curriculum and the teaching'(p.2) — it is not a matter of importing new material but of reviewing the selection of the present content and teaching methods to ensure that both might contribute fully to spiritual and moral development and thus to the development of the whole pupil.

So, what do we mean by spiritual development and by moral development? How can we speak of each in an educational context, and what implications do the notions of spiritual and moral development have for our work in the classroom?

Spiritual Development

A recent OFSTED Report on *Religious Education and Collective Worship* (1994) included this statement:

> More attention needs to be given to the way in which spiritual development might be promoted. For this to happen, schools need to have a shared vocabulary which will help to advance their understanding of how spiritual development is promoted within the school (p.38).

What then can form the basis of our shared vocabulary in terms of 'spiritual development'?

The OFSTED Framework for Inspection made a bold attempt to describe the spiritual area:

Spiritual development relates to that aspect of inner life through which pupils acquire insights into their personal existence which are of enduring worth. It is characterised by reflection, the attribution of meaning to experience, valuing a non-material dimension to life and intimations of an enduring reality. 'Spiritual' is not synonymous with ''religious'; all areas of the curriculum may contribute to pupils' spiritual development' (OFSTED, 1993).

This definition of spiritual development raises significant issues. Spiritual development relates to the personal, the inner life, and the acquisition of insights into experience. It also relates to valuing a non-material dimension to life — a value often alien to many of our pupils! We might consider just how they could discover this 'new world' in the classroom. Another characteristic of spiritual development is reflection, and here we must question what reflection means — (eg. focused thought or attention?) — and whether reflection is natural to all beings or a skill to be developed? And spiritual development is cross-curricular: provision for it involves all curriculum areas. Here then, a relationship is implied between the development of the individual pupil and the experiences offered by the school. There seem to be two key areas in our curriculum planning which we need to consider: firstly, the content needs to raise issues of personal experience, and secondly, our methodology, which needs to encourage questioning of and reflection upon our ways of viewing the world.

To explore more deeply, we might turn to the aspects of spiritual development cited in the National Curriculum Council Discussion Paper. The paper cites eight interrelated aspects (p.2-3), each one strongly affective as well as cognitive and related to a search for values and a sense of meaning and purpose in life. Considered in isolation, they might easily be seen as abstractions, but viewed in relation to specific curriculum areas and activities, they can be seen as the essence of human experience, captured particularly in literature and the arts.

Recognising the value of relationships and a *search for meaning in life* at times of personal suffering may both sound grandiose, yet both lie at the heart of stories such as Raymond Brigg's *Grandpa, The Snowman* and *Badger's Parting Gifts* by S. Varley, all picture books designed for use with infant and junior pupils and all recounting profound relationships touched by a sense of loss. In *Badger's Parting Gifts,* for example, the feelings of sadness and loss experienced by his friends at Badger's death are redeemed by the sharing of their memories of the joyful times they spent with Badger and of his 'gifts', namely the 'skills' they had learnt from him. For secondary pupils, the tragic struggle of Shakespeare's King Lear to grasp the meaning and positive expression of loving reflects both concepts.

A sense of awe, wonder and mystery inspired by the natural world leads us to relive those moments when we have been 'stopped in our tracks' at the sight of a sunset or a rainbow or driven snow, at the birth of a baby or the death of a friend. *Experiencing feelings of transcendence* may for some relate to a *belief* in a divine being, while for others it will be the power of the human spirit to transcend seemingly insurmountable challenges. Brian Keenan's *An Evil Cradling* is a prime example, while the diary of Anne Frank and the novels of Michelle Magorian (eg. *Goodnight Mister Tom*) can be read by pupils across the primary/secondary phase. Reading such novels or enacting drama and questioning when you might have felt like that, and what you might have done had you been one of the characters, encourages the development of *self-knowledge* and the *exploration of feelings and emotions* through consideration of the 'outer' events and 'inner' experiences. These experiences may also be stimulated through listening to music or engaging creatively with visual art.

A key focus for such work in schools is that it fosters an ability to 'reflect', the development of focused thought, upon — usually — human experience. It engages and develops each individual yet draws upon the experiences of the whole group. Both the NCC and OFSTED Discussion Papers acknowledge that individual progress can be made in terms of spiritual development but recognise that this may well not be linear, and both agree that this aspect of personal development can not and will not be inspected.

Moral Development

In an attempt to define moral development, the OFSTED Framework states that 'moral development refers to pupils' knowledge, understanding, intentions, attitudes and behaviour in relation to what is right or wrong.'

The statement poses a number of questions for consideration. Firstly, the use of the terms 'right' and 'wrong' and their links with the term, moral must lead us to question whether we are talking, or should talk, about moral absolutes in an educational setting, and if so, whose moral values should be represented? A controversial issue and one posited by the OFSTED Discussion Paper in two ways. It is envisaged that pupils will develop a sense of morality and, as they do so...

> pupils should become more able to explore the place of reason in ethical matters and, as autonomous moral agents, acquire value-systems which are their own (rather than simply transmitted by others and accepted uncritically), together with the understanding that their behaviour and actions should derive from these beliefs and values.

The aim then is that pupils should develop into autonomous moral agents, able to make reasoned judgements and able to relate their inner beliefs to outward actions.

This may be the ultimate aim of moral development, but how are pupils to make the journey to moral maturity? Both the NCC and OFSTED Papers suggest that schools need to provide a 'moral framework' to guide the pupils in the early stages of their development. This 'moral framework' is seen as consisting of moral values such as 'telling the truth', 'respecting the rights and property of others', 'helping those weaker than ourselves' and 'taking personal responsibility for one's action'. These and other such moral values might be made explicit in schools' Mission Statements but what is not clear is exactly how they are to be recommended or 'enforced' within a school, or how a pupil might develop from one who observes an agreed set of moral values into an 'autonomous moral agent'. We could consult Piaget's or Kohlberg's theories of moral development — or return to our original definition of moral development.

A second question raised by the definition is that moral development involves pupils' knowledge and understanding, and here we might speculate what these terms mean in relation to moral development. Perhaps, taken together, the terms might refer to the ability to recognise a moral dilemma when one is present, an understanding which enables the individual to identify the key influences on the differing standpoints, to know what counts as evidence and the skills to weigh the evidence and arrive at a personal judgement which is consistent with one's individual beliefs and values. This poses the question: how might this ability and these skills be developed in the classroom? Pupils are better able to make moral judgements the more able they are to imagine the consequences of their behaviour, for themselves and for others. Thus, the more opportunities pupils have to encounter controversial issues, to explore different beliefs, to experience decision-making and to reflect upon possible outcomes, the greater are the opportunities for developing moral imagination and skills in moral decision-making.

The material or context for these processes might, in the primary school, emanate from situations related to those values cited within the possible 'moral framework', whether the examples are taken from real life situations at the school, or from a story or the media. In the secondary school, the curriculum itself provides a wealth of opportunities for confronting moral issues at a level appropriate to the age and ability of the pupils. Such controversial issues might include attitudes to the environment, to family relationships and to peace and conflict. For these issues to serve in the moral development of both primary and secondary pupils, they must be treated as 'controversial' and open to investigation and debate, rather than presented in a descriptive manner, open only to a passive acceptance of 'facts'.

A methodology which encourages open debate can leave us as teachers feeling on 'unsafe' ground and unsure of our role, particularly when popular opinion would like to place us as arbiters of the country's morals. It is a very real dilemma for any teacher, and a dilemma explored by the OFSTED Discussion Paper:

> If teachers are not to abuse a position of trust and respect, they surely need to exercise great care and sensitivity in handling controversial moral issues, in order to ensure that their own views are not imposed in a manner which risks coming periously close to indoctrination. Yet if teachers do not take a clear and consistent stand on questions of morality, schools can lack the necessary strengths of a strong ethos and tone.' (OFSTED, 1994, p.11-12)

This is obviously a question of fine balance and is a matter which requires discussion by the staff and senior management in both primary and secondary schools.

Identifying Opportunities for Spiritual and Moral Development

Teaching Spiritual and Moral Development does not necessarily mean importing new teaching material. The NCC Discussion Paper suggests that teachers might capitalise on a variety of learning opportunities, usually inherent within current teaching programmes, to promote pupils' spiritual and moral development. The learning opportunities cited by the Paper (1993) provide the basis for consideration here. Although presented in a linear form, they are closely inter-related. These experiences provide opportunities for pupils to:

- discuss matters of personal concern:
  eg. opportunities to discuss family, local and national conflicts, feelings of loss and grief, alongside those of joy which spring from story or life experience. Language, Literature, Drama, Social Studies and Geography might be involved here.

- develop relationships with adult and peers:
  eg. opportunities for meeting a range of adults from within and outside the school community can emanate from cross-curricular local studies, topics involving RE, History, Geography and English. Shared and even controversial discussion can foster a sense of interdependency within a community, which transcends age-range and personal perspective.

- develop a sense of belonging to a community:
  this is invariably an aim for the school as a community and also in terms of the school's relationship with the wider community. A community is for all its members and this can stimulate discussions on equality of opportunity. One primary class discussed the competing needs of the community, while studying the use of the local park which was under threat of redevelopment. A secondary school explored the breaking down and reformation of community, in a study of the London Dockland Development. In both instances, it was powerful personal case studies which stimulated reflection on the importance of place to the individual and to communities and on the morality of desecrating those places. Both studies incorporated Geography, History and English, and addressed the cross-curricular

themes of the Environment, Citizenship and Economic and Industrial Understanding.

- be challenged by exploring the beliefs and values of others while deepening their knowledge and understanding of their own faith and beliefs:

  RE is a ready forum for exploring beliefs and values, particularly within the local community, but Geography can also be concerned with beliefs and values, as in the two studies mentioned. History too, particularly in studies such as the Second World War, can raise issues related to beliefs in a religious sense and in a broader context of exploring religious and racial prejudice. What is important is that an 'objective' subject of study then provides a forum within which to ask: 'What about you? Where do you stand on this issue?' Too frequently, studies in RE, History and Geography have remained at a descriptive level and have not capitalised on opportunities to challenge pupils' personal responses.

- discuss religious and philosophical questions:

  RE and Science both lend themselves to discussion of ethical issues. Of particular interest to pupils in the secondary school are those related to advanced technology and medical ethics.

- understand why people reach certain decisions on spiritual and moral issues, and how those decisions affect their lives:

  this relates closely with the above, but can be explored most usefully with pupils through individual case studies, maybe of the famous, such as Mother Theresa, but also of the charity workers currently working in danger zones, or of religious groups who do not support the notion of blood transfusions. Television broadcasts frequently include personal case study material, but case studies can also be gained from members of the local community asked to speak about issues of personal concern.

- experience what is aesthetically challenging:

  the Arts have a powerful effect on us and pupils need opportunities to come into contact with a rich variety of art, films, photography, poetry and literature to challenge our stereotypes and lead us to new visions of the world. The vision of the world promoted by *The Animals of Farthing Wood* by C. Dann, would present an excellent starting-

point for primary pupils. Similarly, a study of current press photography from war-torn zones would provide a powerful means of
raising key questions with older pupils.

- experience silence and reflection:
this brings us back to OFSTED's definition of spiritual development,
where 'reflection' was a particular characteristic. Yet schools are
frequently characterised by bustle and business, by noise and frequent
changes of room and activity. Time for some reassessment here.

Monitoring Spiritual and Moral Development

The inspection of spiritual and moral development, together with social
and cultural development, constitutes a quarter of the OFSTED Inspection
Report for a school. So it is vital for schools to take stock of the *provision*
for this area of personal development already present in the general ethos
of the school, encapsulated in the school Mission Statement, in the
planned curriculum for all subjects and in the school's collective worship.
Inspectors will be looking for evidence of such provision and of expected
outcomes in terms of pupils' learning, their behaviour, their attitudes and
values, both in and outside the classroom. Evidence of a planned
programme by which the school is beginning to monitor for itself its
provision and the outcomes demonstrates a positive commitment to the
personal development of its pupils.

Conclusion: A Story

The Whales' Song by Dyan Sheldon and Gary Blythe is a picture book to
be read by all children from 5 to 50 years — and beyond! It is a story
about a young girl, Lilly, her grandmother, her Uncle Frederick — and
about whales.

Lilly's grandmother told her a story.
'Once upon a time', she said, 'the ocean was filled with whales. They
were as big as the hills. They were as peaceful as the moon. They were
the most wondrous creatures you could ever imagine.
'There were whales here millions of years before there were ships, or
cities ...' continued Lilly's grandmother. 'People used to say they were
magical.'

'People used to eat them and boil them down for oil,' grumbled Lilly's Uncle Frederick. And he turned his back and stomped out to the garden.

Just as most 'good' stories encapsulate basic 'truths', so this vignette from *The Whales' Song* encapsulates many, if not all, of the basic issues related to spiritual and moral development. Firstly, both spiritual and moral development focus on relationships, our relationship with ourselves, our relationships with others and our relationship with the natural world. In the extract above, Lilly's grandmother is telling a story about her 'vision' of the world to her granddaughter. She speaks about her relationship with, and response to, the whales, part of the natural world. Secondly, spiritual and moral development requires a context — a story, an issue or an experience which is open to discussion and/or reflection. Here, it is the grandmother's story which provides the context. Thirdly, this context may well be controversial; there may well be different points of view, different visions of the world and this is certainly so when Uncle Frederick comes on the scene. It is he, with his conflicting vision, who confronts us with questions about who is right and who is wrong, where we stand, and what our relationship is with the natural environment. There are no immediately available and clear-cut answers; we are engaged in a process of debate.

When this is the case, what often happens in the classroom is a peculiar mixture of lively debate and quiet individual and communal reflection. And finally, in engaging with this area of pupils' personal development, we cannot be like Uncle Frederick and 'turn our back and stomp out to the garden' — for that breaks the relationship, diminishes the context within which we can discuss and reflect, and refuses to engage with issues that simply will not go away.

References

Department of Education and Science (1977) *Curriculum 11-16,* HMSO

Education Act 1944, Part 2, para.7

Education Reform Act 1988, Chapter 40, Part 1.2

National Curriculum Council (1993) *Spiritual and Moral Development: A Discussion Paper,* NCC, p.2

OFSTED (1993) *Framework for the Inspection of Schools,* HMSO

OFSTED (1994) *Religious Education and Collective Worship 1992- 1993,* HMSO

OFSTED (1994) *Spiritual, Moral, Social and Cultural Development, Discussion Paper*

Sheldon, D. and Blythe, D. (1993) *The Whales' Song,* Red Fox

Chapter 8

Futures Education: Citizenship for Today and Tomorrow

David Hicks

What is it about 'these times' that we need to take into account if we wish to prepare young people for the future? What is the broader context within which discussion about citizenship should be set? This chapter, whilst keeping the local and immediate very much in mind, explores some of the wider issues that impact on daily life in the late twentieth century. To be a fully responsible citizen in the 1990s and beyond requires that we set local concerns in their global context and that we relate the issues of today to the needs of future generations.

Approaching the millennium

State of the world

As the end of the century approaches, a deeper consciousness begins to stir. Not only are we coming to the end of a last decade and the beginning of a first, we are coming to the end of one century and the beginning of another. Nor is this all, for the year 2001 marks the end of the second millennium and the beginning of the third, momentous times in which to be a citizen of Planet Earth. Although the millennium may be 'merely' a sociotemporal construct, it acts as an important metaphor marking our journey through time. How will we look back on the twentieth century, what do we wish to leave behind? How shall we view the twenty-first century, what do we wish to take forward?

The end of the Cold War and the superpower arms race, the disintegration of the Soviet Union, free elections in South Africa — the times radically change. That which seemed so fixed and unchangeable, the global backdrop of our lives, suddenly shifts. As the fear of nuclear war fades with the passing of the 80s, the UN Earth Summit at Rio in 1992 highlighted the new/old urgent agenda of environmental and development issues. Organisations such as the Worldwatch Institute in Washington chart in detail both the state of the world and the global trends that are shaping our future (Brown et al. 1994).

Yet it is not easy to face the global dilemmas that we see daily on our TV screens. Issues to do with the environment, human rights, poverty, war and peace, also affect our own society and communities. In the same way that people repress or deny what they don't wish to face in their own lives and relationships, so they may also respond to the catalogue of global ills by emotionally switching off. Often the pain is too much to bear and so we deny the seriousness of the problems we face and psychic numbing sets in (Staub and Green, 1992). The responsible citizen, however, knows that 'everywhere' is her backyard and that wherever human suffering occurs it calls for justice.

Images of the future

As well as looking at how we deal with global issues it is also important to consider how we manage time. Where have we come from? Where are we now? Where do we want to get to? How do we view the future, that part of history that we can still change? One of the largest studies of people's views of the future (Ornauer, 1972) found that the ability to think about the wider social future was not very well developed. The future was often seen as synonymous with developments in science and technology for example, rather than human enrichment or social justice. People's images of the future were thus very limited and tended to be pessimistic.

The images that citizens have of the future of their society directly affect what they feel it is worth doing in the present. A hundred years ago, in the 1890s, views of the future were extremely optimistic. The British Empire was at its zenith, technology promised untold benefits, the new century was to be a place of continuous social improvement. Such assumptions were cruelly dashed in the First World War when technology was used to create even more effective ways of killing. The future then became a place of doubt and fear. This was reinforced by the Second World War, the end of which marked the beginning of the superpower arms race. Images of the future became even more bleak and pessimistic, haunted by contemplation of nuclear holocaust.

So it is not surprising if western culture still views the future negatively. Popular films such as *Mad Max, The Terminator*, and *Bladerunner*, or comics such as *Judge Dredd* and *2000 AD*, offer young males a continuous diet of violent, hi-tech futures. The images that a society holds of the future matter because they provide feedback to the present. Elise Boulding (1988) and others argue that images of the future play a crucial role in the evolution of a society, acting like a mirror to reflect its inner state of health. When a society generates only negative images of the future it has lost its vitality and direction. Positive images, on the other hand, can act as beacons to draw a society forward towards achievement of its aspirations.

Young people's views

A central concern of citizenship education, therefore, should be with young people's views of the future. Responsible citizenship is more likely to occur if young people feel some ownership of their community, whether local or global, and if they feel optimistic rather than pessimistic about the possibility of changing things for the better. Yet only a minority of educators have shown an interest in what children think and feel about the future or what the role of education should be in helping to create a more just and equitable world in the twenty-first century.

A scattering of studies over the years have identified many of the young people's concerns. Toffler (1974) describes talking to American teenagers about how they thought the future would be and finding a major dissonance between the expected normality of their personal lives and the apocalyptic nature of the anticipated global scene. During the 1980s, too, young people were often extremely pessimistic, fearing a nuclear war that would mean they had no future. More recently Hutchinson's work in Australia (1993) has revealed widespread 'negativity, helplessness, despondency and even anguish about the anticipated problems facing...society and the world at large' amongst young people.

The most recent UK study to examine young people's hopes and fears for the future is particularly relevant to those with an interest in personal and social education and citizenship in the 1990s (Hicks and Holden, 1995). Children are generally optimistic about their personal futures, hoping for a good job, a good life, good relationships and success at school. They fear bad health, unemployment, money and family problems. They are only cautiously optimistic, however, about the future of their local communities, being particularly concerned about crime, quality of the environment, and access to amenities. In relation to the global future they are more pessimistic. In particular they fear the possibility of war, which comes well above pollution and poverty, their other main concerns.

Citizenship: the broader context

What are the implications of the above for citizenship in our schools? At the very least it reminds us that young people face a double burden, not only grappling with their journey towards adulthood but also dealing with the social, political and environmental problems bequeathed them by their forebears. To help make some sense of such issues, effective citizenship education must relate the personal to the global and the present to the future. Since present concerns and national issues are generally dealt with reasonably well in schools what this means is that the spatial and temporal dimensions of citizenship now need to be extended.

Global connections

The process of globalisation is transforming the existing world order through innumerable linkages and interconnections, from knowledge, trade and finance, to fashion, crime and health. The capitalist world economy built up over the last four centuries benefits the core countries of North America, Western Europe and Japan, whilst actively underdeveloping the countries of the periphery in Africa, Asia and Latin America. On the one hand there are moves towards greater global integration and at the same time increasing fragmentation along both economic and ethnic lines.

Forceful calls for citizenship to focus more clearly on the multicultural and global nature of contemporary society have been made by educators such as Lynch (1992), who has explored the need for, and nature of, such an endeavour in some detail. He argues that teachers must recognise three interdependent levels of citizenship, none of which is effective without the others. The three levels are: local community membership, national citizenship, and international citizenship.

His call for a new paradigm for citizenship stresses six key factors that educators must take into account. These are:

- the growth in the number of democratic governments
- the decline in military confrontation between East and West
- the surge in competition for the world's resources
- the recognition of the catastrophic rapidity of environmental decline
- the search for a means to overcome the poverty of the Third World
- the increasing importance of the international role of education in both North and South.

A wealth of excellent resources exists to ensure that a global perspective is present in the curriculum. Practitioners have, in the last two decades, pioneered a wide range of learning approaches for young people to explore their location in a web of local-global interactions. The work of the World Studies Project at Manchester Metropolitan University, the Centre for Global Education at the University College of Ripon and York St John, and Development Education Centres such as those in Birmingham, Manchester and Leeds, all offer unrivalled support to teachers. Exemplary classroom materials are found for younger children in Fountain (1990), for the middle years in Hicks and Steiner (1989), and for older pupils in Pike and Selby (1988; 1994).

The new paradigm that Lynch (1992) calls for must thus also help young people to answer the questions 'Where are we going and where do we want to get to?' as well as 'Where are we now?'

A futures perspective

The National Curriculum makes few explicit references to the future; they most naturally seem to occur within the cross-curricular themes. The future, which in this context means visions, dreams, hopes, purpose, direction, and creativity, i.e. the heart of the human endeavour, has been marginalised. Whilst on the one hand the National Curriculum entitles pupils to 'preparation for the opportunities, responsibilities and experiences of adult life,' many teachers fail to recognise that the adult lives of children will stretch well into the latter part of the 21st century. We are thus legally bound to prepare them for life in, say, 2050. How can we do this unless exploration of possible futures is an explicit concern in the curriculum?

Helping young people explore both probable futures (those which seem *likely* to happen) and preferable futures (those which we feel *ought* to come about) not only makes life more interesting to them, it is what any healthy democratic society would do to secure a more equitable and just future for its citizens. As Longstreet and Shane (1993) point out:

> While historical hindsight, that is, a knowledge of our educational past, provides a helpful basis for curriculum development, it is even more critical today to acquire what we have labelled 'educated foresight.' This...refers to the ability to understand the future significance of rapidly germinating developments in the techno-social milieu of our times.

As we approach the millennium interest in the future grows. Whereas in the 80s many innovative educators were concerned with the need for a global perspective in the curriculum, attention is turning in the 90s to the equal need for a futures perspective. These issues and concerns are being explored more fully by writers such as Beare and Slaughter (1993) in Australia, Tough (1994) in Canada, and Hicks (1994b) in the UK. The nature of a more future-orientated curriculum is further discussed below.

A sustainable society

In many ways the concerns of socially-critical educators are beginning to converge on the rights of future generations and the nature of the 'good society.' Over the last decade or so, economists, philosophers, international lawyers and others have become increasingly interested in what rights future generations should have. The emerging consensus is that no generation should inherit less natural or human-made wealth than the one before it. This extends the notion of human rights to give citizenship a temporal as well as a spatial focus.

The Earth Summit in Rio also focused concern on the twin issues of environment and development and the need to work towards a more just and ecologically sustainable future. Thus those working in both environmental education and development education are coming together to examine how issues of ecology and inequality are inextricably interrelated. The new MSc in Environmental and Development Education at South Bank University marks one exciting innovation in this field. The urgent need to create a more sustainable society should act as one of the overarching goals for citizenship education.

Orr (1992) highlights the way in which education itself has contributed to the social and environmental problems that we now face:

> Education in the modern world was designed to further the conquest of nature and the industrialisation of the planet. It tended to produce unbalanced, underdimensioned people tailored to fit the modern economy. Postmodern education must have a different agenda, one designed to heal, connect, liberate, empower, create and celebrate. Postmodern education must be life- centred.

What does an education for citizenship look like that is based on such values? How much of citizenship as presently practised encourages teachers and students to ask such questions?

Educating for the future

Futures education

Futures education is part of what some call the 'futures field', a loose, overlapping confederation of researchers, professionals, educators and activists who, in different ways, grapple with a diversity of futures-related issues. Any society that neglects consideration of the trends which are shaping its future, and the sort of long-term future it wishes to create, runs the risk of being absorbed in narcissistic reflection.

If all education is for the future we need to ask 'Where and when is the future specifically explored in education?' The term 'futures education' is thus a short-hand term to remind us that all education needs to include a futures perspective. An education which fails to pay specific attention to the future fails signally to prepare its young people for life as citizens or to ensure its future security.

A socially critical approach

Education is not and never can be neutral, as some would have us believe. All approaches to education are underpinned by specific attitudes, values and ideologies. Jonathon Kozol writes (1980):

> There is no such thing as a 'neutral skill,' nor is there 'neutral education.' Children can learn to read and write in order to understand instructions, dictates and commands. else they can read in order to grasp the subtle devices of their own manipulation — the methods by which a people may be subjugated and controlled...Oppenheimer, working on the final stages of development of the atom bomb, and his co-worker Fermi (said) that they were 'without special competence on the moral question'...It is this, not basic skills but basic competence for basic ethical indignation, which is most dangerously absent in our schools and society today.

If education played a part in creating the global crisis that we now find ourselves in, we need a different sort of education to help us out. In particular we require a socially critical education which helps students explore questions of justice and inequality. Table 1 opposite sets out a possible agenda.

Questions such as these should lie at the heart of democratic education (Hicks, 1994a). If children are to grow up to become empowered and responsible citizens, it will be because they have learnt and practised these skills at school.

Citizenship for tomorrow

Three glimpses of what a more future-orientated education for citizenship might look like are given below. Firstly, a series of questions are raised in relation to some of the main themes within citizenship. Secondly, an example is given of a classroom activity for exploring interrelationships between past, present and future in society. Thirdly, attention is drawn to the work of one particular curriculum project which specifically helps older pupils to consider different scenarios for the future of Britain.

Table 1 — Education for justice

1. *What is the issue?*

What do we think, feel, hope and fear, in relation to this particular issue? What do others who are involved think, feel and say?

2. *How has it come about?*

Why do we and others think, feel and act the way we do? What and who has influenced us and others involved? What is the history of this situation?

3. *Who gains, who loses?*

Who has the power in this situation and how do they use it? Is it used to the advantage of some and the disadvantage of others? If so, in what way?

4. *What is our vision?*

What would things look like in a more just, peaceful and sustainable future, for ourselves and for others? What values will we use to guide our choices?

5. *What can be done?*

What are the possible courses of action open to us? What are others already doing? Which course of action is most likely to achieve our vision of a preferred future?

6. *How will we do it?*

How shall we implement our plan of action in school, at home, or in the community? How shall we work together? Whose help might we need? How do we measure our success?

Questions to be asked

How might one ensure that citizenship education will really help prepare young people for tomorrow today? The questions in Table 1 relate to the critical pedagogy that such an education requires. The questions set out in Table 2 opposite refer to the eight components of citizenship proposed in Curriculum Guidance 8 (1990). They are intended to make more explicit the futures dimension that is already inherent in citizenship education (Hicks, 1994a).

The 200 Year Present

This activity is one of a variety (Hicks 1994a) aimed at helping children to explore the relationships between past, present and future. Although framed somewhat in personal terms here, it can be varied to highlight a range of social, cultural and democratic processes.

Procedure

Introduce the class to Elise Boulding's idea of the extended two hundred year present (Table 3). The class is going to explore its own such present through talking to parents and grandparents, or other older relations and neighbours, and anticipating the lives of their own future children and grandchildren.

It is useful to have pictures or illustrations that help children visualise these relationships, e.g. five human figures across a two hundred year timescale with the present year in the centre. From left to right these figures could be labelled: grandparent, parent, myself, my child, my grandchild. Actual or approximate dates of birth could be put under each.

These relationships can be explored in a variety of ways. For example:

— Interviewing parents, relations or other adults about what life was like when they were children. How was society different, how the same?

— Interview a grandparent or older relative/neighbour about what their childhood was like. How was it different from/the same as their own/their parents' childhood?

— What were the most important events in their parents' and grandparents' (or others') lives? What were the biggest changes

Table 2 — Citizenship for the future

Community — What sort of community would we ideally like to live in? What examples are there from the past of people trying to create their ideal community? What do we need to do in order to create a better community now and in the future?

A pluralist society — What hopes and fears for the future do different ethic and cultural groups in Britain have? What does a future society based on racial justice and equality actually look like? What needs to be done to achieve it?

Being a citizen — What does global citizenship look like and how does it relate to the global community? What rights and responsibilities should we have in the future? What rights should future generations have?

The family — What might the family look like in the future? What are the advantages and disadvantages of different forms of relating? How should we prepare for our future roles as parents and partners?

Democracy in action — What would a participatory democracy look like, in school, in the community, and nationally? How can we really experience this? How might democracy evolve in the future?

The citizen and the law — What new legislation might be needed in order to create a more just and sustainable future? Who would benefit from this? Who might resist such legislation?

Work, employment and leisure — What sort of work and leisure would we like in the future? What sort of work, and what sort of leisure activities, promote environmental concern?

Public services — What existing services support our visions of a better community? What new services are needed to help bring our preferable futures about? How might they be provided?

Table 3 — The extended present

(This is) a medium range of time, which is neither too long or too short for immediate comprehension, and which has an organic quality that gives it relevance for the present moment. This medium range is the 200-year present. That present begins 100 years ago today, on the day of birth of those among us who are centenarians. Its other boundary is the hundredth birthday of the babies born today. This present is a continuously moving moment, always reaching out a hundred years in either direction from the day we are in. We are linked with both boundaries of this moment by the people among us whose life began or will end at one of those boundaries, five generations each way in time. It is our space, one that we can move around indirectly in our own lives and indirectly by touching the lives of the young and old around us (Boulding, 1988).

---

seen by each generation? A collage can be made to illustrate these changes.

— Are there any special stories or objects that have been passed down in their families?

This sort of activity may well be familiar to pupils from work in History. What makes it different is the second half of the sequence — looking to the future — which is equally essential.

— How do pupils think the world might be different when they are old age pensioners? When will this be?

— What objects, qualities, wishes would they like to pass on to their children and grandchildren?

— Pupils write a letter to one of their future grandchildren telling them i) what their own life is like today and ii) in what ways they hope their world will be better in the future.

— In how many different ways are these generations related? What do they pass on to each other? Pupils may initially think of objects being handed down, but also handed down are traditions, human rights and responsibilities.

— Do we have a responsibility to help future generations, e.g. our children and grandchildren? What might we do now that they would be grateful for in the future?

While it may be easier to explore the last hundred years, the next hundred equally demand our attention. We need to develop pupil skills of anticipation, the understanding that decisions made now have effects far into the future, and that we have a responsibility to future generations.

Choices for Britain 2003

The Choices for Britain Project (Public Voice International, 1994), which has been piloted in Avon, is designed for the 14-18 age group and particularly aimed at developing students' discussion and communication skills. To start with students are presented with some key facts and background information about Britain in the 20th century and in relation to the European Community and the United Nations today. They are also given a range of opinions about possible threats to Britain's future, e.g. problems at home, environmental problems, Britain's declining power, poverty in the world, conflicts and wars.

Subsequently students consider four different scenarios for the future of Britain in 2003. These are entitled: Great Britain, Euro-Britain, Global Britain and Island Britain. For each future scenario they are given brief information on what critics and supporters say about it, whether this future is realistic, and how much it would cost. Descriptions of two of the scenarios are given in Table 4.

A range of activities follow which encourage students to consider the different steps that would be necessary to reach any of the four futures. Finally, they are invited to complete a short questionnaire to indicate what a fifth future, their future for Britain would look like. Some of the questions they are invited to consider are:

— What do you believe are the most important problems facing Britain and the world?

— What kind of a country would you like Britain to be in ten years' time?

155

Table 4 — Choices for Britain

Great Britain

It is 2003. Over the past ten years, we have come to understand that the UK still has a special role to play in the world as an active and independent country. We are taking an active role in promoting freedom, democracy and fair play in other countries, for we know that Britain has a special responsibility to make the world a better place. We have kept our armed forces the same size and we send them to other countries when we feel we must, to help keep the peace. At home, we have worked hard to make our country's economy stronger. The rest of Europe may be working towards having common armed forces, a common foreign policy, and a common currency, but we know that there would be more to lose than to gain by joining a United Europe. It would get us too involved in their own problems and prevent us from doing whatever we wanted around the world. So we have kept our freedom of action, though we continue to co-operate and do business with the rest of Europe. In 2003, we are a proud and powerful country, respected by our neighbours. We have made Britain great again.

Global Britain

It is 2003. Over the past ten years, we have come to understand that the world's problems are our problems. We knew that if the UK didn't do more about the growing poverty, pollution and conflicts in other parts of the world, and encourage other countries to do more too, these problems would seriously threaten us. To help narrow the gap between rich and poor countries, Britain now spends a great deal more each year on development assistance. We have also decided to forget about the money that many developing countries owe us. For a fairer world, we encourage the United States, Japan and other developed countries to allow developing countries more of a say in how the world is run. We work closely with the UN on global problems, and often provide our troops to help the UN keep the peace where there are conflicts. And we never use our own troops unless the UN approves. At home, we use our cars less and pay heavy taxes on products that cause pollution. Bananas and other foods from developing countries cost more, now that we are paying their farmers a fairer price. In 2003, Britain is working towards a bright new future for the world

(From Hicks and Holden, 1995.)

— Why would some people not like your future, and how would you respond to them? What are some good points about your future?

Looking forwards

This chapter has argued that education for citizenship must include both a global and a futures perspective if it is to be relevant to the needs of the 21st century. As the millennium approaches we may be faced with a choice between global collapse or a more sustainable future (Meadows, 1992). Although many books on education and citizenship now include reference to European and international concerns, few demonstrate the necessary global and multicultural perspectives highlighted by Lynch (1992). Even fewer espouse a socially critical approach to learning, or focus on the hopes and fears that children themselves have for the future.

Any curriculum that is to prepare students for the 1990s and beyond must include both a global and a futures dimension. Whilst citizenship can play an important part in developing this dimension, it must also be a matter of whole-school policy and the resources to achieve this are increasingly becoming available. In his challenge to the Great Education Reform Bill, Robin Richardson (1988) described in this acrostic, aspects of the education that we need for the future:

Girl-friendly and generous
Equality focused and empowering
Racial justice generating and renewing
Beauty begetting and birthing
Identity-strengthening and illumining
Life and love-centred and liberating.

David Orr (1993) completed the picture when he wrote:

Students in the next century will need to know how to create a civilisation that runs on sunlight, conserves energy, preserves biodiversity, protects soils and forests, develops sustainable local economies and restores the damage inflicted on the Earth. In order to achieve such ecological education we need to transform our schools and universities.

These are the real challenges for those involved in education for citizenship and indeed for all concerned educators wherever they may be.

References

Beare, H. and Slaughter, R. (1993) *Education for the Twenty- First Century,* London, Routledge

Boulding, E. (1988) *Building a Global Civic Culture: Education for an Interdependent World,* New York, Teachers College Press

Brown, L. et al. (1994) *State of the World 1994,* London, Earthscan Publications

Fountain, S. (1990) *Learning Together: Global Education 4-7,* Cheltenham, Stanley Thornes

Hicks, D. (1994a) *Educating for the Future: A Practical Classroom Guide,* Godalming, World Wide Fund for Nature UK

Hicks, D. ed. (1994b) *Preparing for the Future: Notes and Queries for Concerned Educators,* London, Adamantine Press

Hicks, D. and Steiner, M. (eds) (1989) *Making Global Connections: A World Studies Workbook,* Edinburgh, Oliver and Boyd1,

Hicks, D. and Holden, C. (1995) *Visions of the Future: Why we Need to Teach for Tomorrow,* Stoke-on-Trent, Trentham Books

Hutchinson, F. (1993) 'Educating beyond fatalism and impoverished social imagination: are we actively listening to young people's voices on the future?' *Peace, Environment and Education, 4 (4),* 36-57

Kozol, J. (1980) *The Night is Dark and I am Far From Home,* New York, Continuum

Longstreet, W. and Shane, H. (1993) *Curriculum for a New Millennium Boston, Allyn and Bacon*

Lynch, J. (1992) *Education for Citizenship in a Multicultural Society,* London, Cassell

Meadows, D. and Randers, J. (1992) *Beyond the Limits:* Global Collapse or a Sustainable Future, London, Earthscan

National Curriculum Council (1990) *Education for Citizenship:* Curriculum Guidance 8, York, NCC

Ornauer, H. et al. (1976) *Images of the World in the Year 2000,* Atlantic Highlands, NJ, Humanities Press

Orr, D. (1992) *Ecological Literacy: Education and the Transition to a Postmodern World,* Albany, State University of New York Press

Orr, D. (1993) 'Schools for the 21st century,' *Resurgence,* No. 160, September/October

Public Voice International (1993) *Choices for Britain: Teacher's Guide,* 82 Colston Street, Bristol BS1 5BB

Pike, G. and Selby, D. (1988) *Global Teacher, Global Learner,* London, Hodder and Stoughton

Pike, G. and Selby, D. (1994) *Reconnecting: From National to Global Curriculum,* Godalming, World Wide Fund for Nature UK

Richardson, R. (1988) Opposition to reform and the need for transformation. *Multicultural Teaching* Vol.6 No.2, Spring

Staub, S. and Green, P. (1992) *Psychology and Social Responsibility: Facing Global Challenges,* New York, New York University Press

Toffler, A. (1974) *Learning for Tomorrow: The Role of the Future in Education,* New York, Vintage Books

Tough, A. (1994) *Crucial Questions About the Future,* London, Adamantine Press

Chapter 9

The future basis for a 14-19 Entitlement?

Michael Young

1. Introduction

This book has two bold and related aims. First it re-asserts the idea that education is not just about access to the basic areas of specialist knowledge and understanding (nor in its later phases, to learning the skills and knowledge appropriate to specific jobs); it is also *and more fundamentally* concerned with the personal and social development of students as future adults and citizens. This idea itself is of course not new. It can be found in most books on educational philosophy and (as the editors of this book remind us), it was enshrined in the 1944 Education Act as well as the Acts of 1988 and 1992. However, nineteen years after James (now Lord) Callaghan's Ruskin Speech which criticised teachers for giving too much attention to the personal development of students, and when almost every Department for Education White Paper in the last decade has been about improving Britain's economic competitiveness, the role of the school in promoting the personal and social development of pupils needs re-asserting.

Secondly, in the wake of National Curriculum Orders, League Tables and National Targets, this book reasserts the importance of individual schools taking control of their own curriculum. It is the link between these two ideas that is important and it is expressed in two arguments. Firstly 'a pupil's personal development must..(lie) at the centre of whole curriculum planning... (and) at the heart of a school's purpose and rationale'. Secondly, if this is to be more than well- intentioned rhetoric, both the *outcomes* (in terms of curriculum purposes) and the *processes* (in terms of pedagogy or teaching and learning) of personal and social development have to be made explicit on the basis of a shared set of values. In tackling personal development issues in this specific way, the authors recognise that pupils are not some general class-free, gender- free and non-ethnic category dreamed up in the minds of traditional liberal educators; in this book pupils are living persons with class, gender and cultural identities. In other words the book is a practical recognition of the inescapably moral and political character of education.

In this chapter, I begin by exploring further the notion of whole curriculum planning and its implications both for the organisation of schools and the role of teachers. Next, two issues are introduced that are not explicitly discussed in the previous chapters about the contexts of schools. The first is the growing tendency for the majority of pupils to continue in full time study after 16, together with the increasing divergence between pre- and post- 16 educational provision. The second issue is the implications of global economic changes and how they may require us to rethink the relationship between what have traditionally been seen as the separate educational goals of personal development preparation for employment. Finally, I suggest that in arguing for personal and social development to be at the core of the role of schools, we are led to re- conceptualise the curriculum as a whole and, more fundamentally, to begin to rethink the relationship between schools, as specialist 'organisations for learning', and society. There is much written recently about the advent of a learning society and how it is made up of learning organisations. This means that more and more organisations are taking on an explicit *educational* role and gearing their concepts of personal and social development to their particular ends. If this is so we will need to consider what this means for schools which claim that their concepts of personal and social development are not just another set of goals but goals that represent the future of the society as a whole.

2. Personal and Social Development and whole school curriculum policies

The editors of this book interpret the OFSTED guidelines as recognising that establishing personal and social development as a curriculum goal does not mean a new subject on the timetable but a set of criteria for the curriculum as a whole. In other words the argument is that it is *whole schools*, not just individual class or year tutors or those with special responsibility for personal and social development, that need to reassess the curriculum from the perspective of the personal development of all their pupils. However, if this is to be more than a rhetorical recommendation that can do little more than remind all teachers to bear some criteria in mind, a new approach to the curriculum is required that changes the relationship between personal development goals, the educational aims of school subjects and a school's whole curriculum goals. Such a new approach to the curriculum does not necessarily involve changes in the National Curriculum itself (though the narrowness and bias of the compulsory component of key stage 4 remains a problem). It is a question of how individual schools define their curriculum purposes and how their specialist subject teaching is developed in relationship to the purposes of the school as a whole.. Such an approach is a radical inversion of current practice when the demands of subject teaching tend to dominate all other school goals. Schools will need to know how each of their activities contributes to the overall curriculum goals of the school. This will require them to develop a *collective intelligence* (Brown and Lauder, 1995) about all their activities, many of which can be treated by subject departments and others with specific responsibilities as almost their private property.

In order to make more concrete what might be involved in such changes, I want to distinguish between two ways in which schools might organise their curriculum. I shall describe these as *bureaucratic* and *connective* integration (Young, 1993: Young, et al, 1994) and argue that while bureaucratic integration will inevitably leave personal and social development at the margin of a school's curriculum priorities, connective integration requires the personal and social development of pupils to be one of its core principles. I shall suggest that despite the external and internal pressures to maintain (or even to revert to) the bureaucratic model, there are not only powerful reasons for change, but signs that even within the bureaucratic model interim strategies are emerging which exhibit some of the features of connectivity.

3. Curriculum Model(1): Bureaucratic integration

It is first necessary to outline what I mean by *bureaucratic* integration. The traditional secondary school curriculum (expressed clearly in the National Curriculum, though less so in the latest Dearing version) was based on relatively autonomous subjects, taught in departments and managed by a Head and Deputies (who divided their responsibilities by separating control of the timetable from responsibility for discipline and pastoral care). Once the timetable was decided, there was very little that different subject teachers needed to discuss together; everything was decided in departments. In other words it was a centrally co-ordinated, and delegated curriculum (not unlike the organisation of production in many factories of the post war years).

The advent of TVEI and the many other curriculum developments of the 1980s put this model under strain. A whole variety of new posts for assessment, careers, Records of Achievement and vocational education had to be created. The principle was of adding on to a subject-led curriculum and the whole was, literally, 'the sum of the parts' and no more. Any 'added value' (to the subjects) was implicit rather than explicit and, not surprisingly, many subject teachers saw the encroachment of tutorial guidance or other non-subject activities as an encroachment on 'real learning time'. No less surprising was that the whole range of learner support and non-subject-based activities, together with much of the pastoral and personal development activities should become associated with the low achievers. New divisions appeared in secondary schools. Subject specialists either felt threatened by these non-subject curriculum developments or dismissed them as only appropriate for lower ability pupils who could not cope with 'real' subject learning (Spours and Young, 1988). On the other hand, those who promoted the idea of a personal development curriculum often dismissed school subjects as elitist and 'alienating' for the majority of pupils. Bureaucratic integration was therefore the organisational basis for one of the major divisions within secondary education — that between the pastoral and the subject curriculum(Power, 1991) — and was a precursor of academic/vocational divisions after 16. A major problem of the Dearing key stage 4 proposals is that linking greater freedom for schools to a narrow compulsory core and optional GNVQs could lead to an even more rigid version of that divide beginning at 14.

The bureaucratic model of curriculum integration has two implications for personal and social development (PSD) as a curriculum goal. Firstly, as a curriculum model based on separate subjects, the curriculum aim of PSD is marginalised. Secondly, PSD is dependent on the chance commitment of individual teachers and is likely to reappear in the form of social and life skills for low achievers, as a replacement for the mainstream curriculum from which they have been excluded.

Schools are not immune to modernising tendencies and there are signs that the bureaucratic model is being pushed to its limits. Since the 1988 Act and especially since the establishment of National Targets and League Tables, schools have been under increasing pressure to be more 'effective' in terms of the numbers and levels of qualifications that pupils achieve. The focus on institutional effectiveness has undermined some of the autonomy of subject departments by encouraging academic tutoring and the monitoring of individual pupil attainment. Such developments represent a shift in some features of the bureaucratic model in that they stress the integrative role of the ethos of a school and the sharing of goals rather than relying largely on a hierarchical structure. One of the limitations of most approaches to school effectiveness is that, despite claims made to the contrary, they take the purposes of a school as given. In doing so, they draw on an *organisational* rather than a *curriculum* view of ethos (i), leaving the content, pedagogy and relations between subjects that are associated with the old model unchanged.

Furthermore, a top-down approach to improving effectiveness can be resented (and therefore resisted) by teachers and may impinge only indirectly on students as learners. Such approaches are concerned with making existing organisational structures operate more effectively and therefore do not address the possibility that it may be these structures themselves that are part of the problem. The old model of bureaucratic integration was associated with maintaining internal hierarchies and the role of the school in the wider processes of social selection. The demands on schools to raise the attainment *of all pupils* by involving students in the management of their own learning are in direct contradiction to this. It may be that it is in this contradiction between external demands and internal structures that we can identify the sources of change and the connections between organisational structures and the issue of personal and social development.

There is, however another factor at work, to which I return later. Creating incentives for change, depends on finding ways of developing a sense of purpose, linked to new possibilities for the future, for both teachers and pupils. Present government policy assumes that purpose for individuals can be left to individual choice and that for institutions it can be left to the market and fear of competition. However even successful businesses, on which it is assumed such 'market' ideas are based, need a vision of what people might need in the future.

4. Curriculum Model (2); Connective Integration

I suggested earlier that a model for integrating personal and social development into the curriculum as a whole would invert much current practice; the connective model does this in two ways. Firstly, it does not start with the National Curriculum but with the curriculum purposes of individual schools (and in some cases consortia). Secondly, it does not start from subject areas but from educational purposes. A school would define its purposes in terms of the kind of young person, adult, worker, citizen, and parent that, in discussion with parents, it wants its pupils to become and the kind of knowledge, skills and attitudes that it envisages that they will need when they leave school to fulfil such roles. Instead of treating the National Curriculum as something imposed on schools, such a school would interpret it as a way of providing a broad specification of content that ensures that student learning does not become school-specific and therefore has currency across the country. Many of the specific areas of personal and social development that would be involved in a school's own curriculum purposes are described in earlier chapters of this book. The point here is that in a connective model, personal and social development becomes one of the sets of criteria a school uses for interpreting the National Curriculum Orders, choosing Examination Boards and using the discretion allowed to it, especially at key stage 4.

For individual schools, two steps are crucial in moving towards such a model. First, all staff would need to endorse the common criteria and be required to articulate how their subjects would be involved in both supporting the processes and in delivering the *outcomes*. Secondly, the criteria would be used by subject (and other) specialist staff to develop assignments and learning plans and feed back this process to a school's curriculum committee. The model is connective in the sense that subject specialists have to *connect* their subject teaching to (a) the overall school curriculum purposes and (b) the way other subjects are contributing to whole-school curriculum criteria. The role of subjects would need to be made explicit in two ways: firstly their role in the whole curriculum would need to identified in terms of the kind of skills and knowledge young people would be likely to need as citizens and workers in the next century, and secondly the contribution that subjects could make to raising overall levels of attainment and achievement.

The school management model needed for delivering a curriculum based on connective integration would be curriculum-led rather than organisation-led and would need to be based on goals defined and agreed by the whole staff. It would be quite different from the combination of hierarchical co-ordination and delegation that characterises the bureaucratic model. Furthermore, quite different relationships would need to be developed between activities that have been traditionally separate and delivered through pastoral and subject curricula: such as subject tutoring, general tutoring and learner support and guidance. Incorporating personal and social development criteria into goals for the whole curriculum as well as ensuring that specialist subject goals are subsidiary to them will not be easy, when subjects are, at least in practice, seen as ends in themselves. For subjects to be *used for* curriculum purposes rather than *used to* define those purposes requires a vision of the future we are aiming to prepare young people for. The National Curriculum, apart from the introduction of compulsory technology, is based on a vision of the past, if it can be said to be based on a vision at all. It is not surprising in such a context that subjects should still be dominant.

5. From bureaucratic to connective integration

What then are the external forces that schools might capitalise on to make such a change happen? Schools are under enormous pressure to be more effective, to make do with less resources and to enable their students to achieve ever better examination results. Mostly this is experienced as top-down and as a bureaucratic and a flawed attempt to impose questionable business principles on schools. I have already pointed to the tensions between these demands and the existing way that schools are organised, particularly as this impacts on teachers as professionals. Teachers do want more of their pupils to reach higher levels and to raise standards of achievement generally and they are aware that the more students feel a sense of ownership of their own learning, the more they will achieve in curriculum terms.

It is for this reason that teachers have responded so positively to the introduction of Recording Achievement and individual Action Planning and to the potential of value-added approaches to institutional improvement. We have in these tendencies an indication that the bureaucratic model, which has been inherited from an earlier era, is increasingly at odds with the pressures to raise overall levels of attainment. Furthermore there is also evidence of the emergence of a transitional approach, less hierarchical and less tied to the separation of subjects, which is directed to supporting pupils in improving their achievements. This change in some elements of the *bureaucratic* model remains based, however, on a traditional view of curriculum and pedagogy involving the transmission of fixed bodies of knowledge to passive learners; a view that has been given extra life by both the content and the form of the National Curriculum. In the strength of its subject divisions, in the relative weakness of its cross curricular (connective) themes and in the form in which it was imposed in its earlier versions, the National Curriculum has provided a boost to the bureaucratic model and made teachers understandably defensive and reluctant to take risks with anything new and untested (Rowe and Whitty, 1993).

Ken Spours and I (Spours and Young, 1995) have recently reported on our work with a group of teachers in developing value-added strategies in VIth Forms and colleges. One of the many lessons from the development work carried out by the teachers involved in the project has been that such strategies lead to students becoming increasingly involved in managing their own learning. It is this outcome, rather than the statistical or recording aspects of value-added approaches that have been the catalyst for bringing together subject and pastoral curricula and for helping subject specialists to see the value of a whole-school or *connective* approach to the curriculum. In the third year of this project we plan to explore with the teachers some of the curriculum implications of taking a value added approach to raising achievement. In contrast to other innovations such as the attempts to reconstruct the whole curriculum in modular form, the value-added approach, with its focus on student learning gain, leads concretely to question of *what learning?* and the potential of basing a school curriculum on the personal and social development of pupils.

6. The changing role of teachers: from insular to connective specialists?

Making personal and social development a whole *school* curriculum priority for all staff places new demands on senior management and teachers, especially those whose training and experience has been as subject specialists. It requires Heads and Deputies to broaden their definitions of school ethos to include not only organisational matters such as staff discipline and morale but also the way different subject departments contribute to the whole curriculum. In other words, Heads will need to take on a curriculum leadership role and not leave subject departments to define their own goals in terms of their separate subjects. Parallel to the emergence of a new role for Heads will be new roles for Heads of department, who will no longer be restricted to their own subjects; they will need to articulate the role of the subjects in the whole curriculum. Teachers of specialist subjects will also have to develop new skills and knowledge as well as new approaches to their subjects and their relationship to the curriculum as a whole. Inevitably such an approach will challenge the professional identity of some subject teachers if this has been based on a bounded or insular knowledge of their subject rather than on how different subjects relate to the goals of the curriculum as a whole.

Traditionally, subject specialists have tended to view the curriculum from the point of view of their subjects as an ends in themselves. From this subject-perspective, personal and social development always appears as something additional to the subject curriculum. As subject syllabuses are always perceived as 'overloaded', such additions will all too easily be seen as taking away time given to subject teaching. However, if subject specialists have a model of the curriculum *as a whole* to which their subject contributes, it becomes possible for them to ask how any specific subject (for example, Physics or English) contributes to a pupil's personal and social development. This need not be seen as diluting a teacher's specialist subject knowledge, but it does involve a redefinition of the role of specialist subject teachers. In the terms used in this chapter, subject teachers have to become *connective* rather than *insular* specialists. When teachers are insular specialists, subject knowledge is used to define teacher roles and keep them apart from each other. The connective subject specialist, however, is someone who has specialist subject knowledge, knows how her/his specialist knowledge relates to the broader purposes of the curriculum and shares a definition of those purposes with other teachers. The move from bureaucratic to connective integration can therefore be seen as the basis for democratising specialist knowledge, enhancing the broader educational role of subject teachers, and extending the range of students who can get access to specialist knowledge.

Inevitably some subject teachers will resist any move away from a model of the curriculum which insulates subject specialisms. They will argue that the content and depth of subject teaching will be undermined and can all too easily point to the weak conceptual content of programmes that are not subject-based. The most obvious examples are social education (Whitty et al, 1994) and prevocational courses (Spours and Young, 1988). Overcoming such resistance is a key issue for Heads, for those responsible for professional development and for higher education institutions involved in teacher training. At the school level connective integration will require all subject teachers to be involved in developing criteria for personal and social development as well as other aspects of the school's whole curriculum, and in suggesting how they may be expressed in different subjects.

7. Continuity and discontinuity at 16+: Towards a 14-19 entitlement

Understandably, the previous chapters of this book focus on the compulsory phase of schooling. However, as the proportion of those who continue to study after 16 continues to rise, the problems of pre/post-16 continuity become more and more acute and it becomes increasingly necessary to treat the pre- and post-16 phases as a continuous whole. Until recently, the organisation of provision for those staying on after 16 assumed it was provision for a minority. This minority was initially the 'academic' VIth former and the day release student at college and then, in the late 1970s, it began to include the 'new' or (one year) VIth Former and the 'new' full time FE student. By the beginning of the 1980s, those staying on in school or college amounted to at most 40% of the cohort. Personal and social development after 16 was ad hoc and informal. In colleges (except VIth Form colleges) it hardly existed. In school VIth Forms it consisted of sports, prefect systems, school trips or societies and sometimes classroom-based activities such as general and liberal studies and debating. In its elite form in the Public Schools this can be seen as a 'curriculum for future leaders', strengthened by the possibilities of extra-curricular social education for students who are in residence. The Public Schools are thus able to compensate for the narrowness of the formal curriculum of three A levels instead of the broad formal curriculum that is typical of upper secondary education on the European continent.

By 1994, the proportion of students staying on after 16 had increased to over 70% of the cohort. The students are split evenly between those remaining at school and those going to Further Education or VIth Form Colleges. Alternative post-16 curricula have been developed, based on the three-track qualification system consisting of A and AS levels, GNVQs and work based NVQs. As many schools and colleges have been under financial pressure to increase pupil/staff ratios, and colleges are funded only for activities linked specifically to qualifications, the personal development curriculum for those over 16 has been neglected, at least outside the Public (and some GM) Schools. A levels have no requirement for personal and social development and GNVQ compulsory core skills are limited to numeracy, communications and use of IT. There are no cross-curricular themes and no common core for all post-16 students that could provide some continuity through the 14-19 phase of education. Some institutions attempt to maintain a personal and social development curriculum through their tutorial system and others through using the ASDAN Youth Award Scheme or the Open College Network.

This picture is in stark contrast to the main systems of provision in continental Europe. Whether provision is based on full-time study as in France or the Nordic countries or, as in Germany, on gymnasia (grammar schools) and an employer-based system of vocational education, there is an explicit curriculum for all students up till 18 or 19, which includes civics and social studies regardless of the line or mode of study that a student follows. Whereas on the continent it is assumed that personal and social development of students continues after compulsory schooling, in England students are assumed to have completed their personal and social development by 16. Perhaps a more accurate view is that the government remains content that the social education of leaders (in Public and some GM Schools) continues on the informal basis of the past, while hoping that the rest will be prepared through vocational courses for their future life as employees. We might contrast this view of preparing the citizens of a democracy with that recommended by Gramsci 60 years ago, when he wrote:

> democracy, by definition, cannot mean merely that an unskilled worker becomes skilled. It must mean that every 'citizen' can 'govern' and that society places him (or her) even if only abstractly, in a general condition to achieve this... (the common school) should therefore ensure that... (every child) up to the threshold of her/his first job, (should have the opportunity to become) *a person capable of thinking, studying and ruling or controlling those who rule.* (my italics)

Like so many important issues in the English education system (it is always important to remember that things are very different in Scotland), the need for a coherent and balanced provision for the whole cohort up to 18 has either been consciously avoided or just has not been thought through. We have had programmes like TVEI which stressed 14-18 continuity and gave rise to ideas like student entitlement and college charters. On the other hand the recent emphasis of government policy has been on student choice, both through the scheme for training credits and by encouraging institutional competition and marketing, rather than on promoting continuity. Without a 14-19 curriculum framework that makes a concept of core curriculum explicit, though with greater flexibility than in the National Curriculum, and without funding strategies that encourage institutional collaboration (to overcome the discontinuities between schools and colleges), it is difficult to see what increasing student-choice could mean, let alone how individual schools and colleges could develop the proposals in this book for students after 16.

Two items in a recent *Times Educational Supplement* (24/2/95) illustrate the problem on a national level. On one page there is a summary of a recently published Royal Society of Arts report arguing for a 14-19 system of learning and including most of the elements of personal and social development included in this book. The proposals are not new and repeat many of the suggestions of the Institute of Public Policy Research in 1990, the Royal Society in 1991 and the National Commission in 1993. At least, however, the issue is kept open and the government is reminded that those arguing for a unified and coherent curriculum framework for the whole 14-19 stage represent a powerful professional consensus that is not going to go away. A previous page of the same paper gives the other side of the picture and reports the announcement by the School Curriculum and Assessment Authority (six months after it took the decision!) that they have abolished their 14-19 Committee. This is at a time when the issue of 14-19 continuity is more urgent than ever. The most recent statistics point to the fact that of the 70+% of the cohort who now continue full time study after 16, half have left two years later. Whereas some of these students will have made positive decisions to take up a job, many will have dropped out without gaining any additional qualifications.

The issues concerning continuity are difficult and the debate about a coherent 14-18 curriculum has hardly begun. Under pressure from increasing fragmentation of programmes and an awareness that staying on in school could be little more than the 'warehousing' of young people before they are returned to the labour market, the concept of a 14-19 curriculum of the future is beginning to emerge. It may be that the dramatic disappearance of youth labour markets (63% of 16 year olds got jobs in 1980, and this had fallen to 9% by 1993) and the no less dramatic increase in staying on after 16 will force those involved in the post-compulsory sector to realise that we face new circumstances which need a new concept of the curriculum. The issues facing those designing the pre-14 curriculum are even are less clear — though David Hicks's chapter in this book gives us some useful pointers. What is certain is that the rhetorical persuasion that is the function of National Targets and the fear of competition and consequent loss of funding are no substitute for serious curriculum thinking. At a level of principle, we could do worse, when thinking of the upper secondary curriculum, than turn again to Gramsci. His view was that the aim of what he described as 'the last phase of the common school' (what we refer to as the 14-18 phase) should be to: 'create (in pupils)...

the intellectual self-discipline and the moral independence which are necessary for subsequent specialisation'. In this view personal and social development is closely linked both to the issue of choice and to the consequences of choice (specialisation).

8. Personal and social development and national economic futures

I mentioned that since Callaghan's Ruskin College speech in 1976, the economic role of education has taken precedence over its role in the personal and intellectual development of young people. The present book represents an important counter to that tendency. This matters not only because of the intrinsic importance of the educational aims that have been neglected and which this book endorses, but also because it reminds us that the economic role of education is far from clear and that there are no unambiguous learning gains to be achieved by trying to link education more closely to economic needs. In fact, those who argue for a more economy-oriented curriculum are often more concerned with political and ideological outcomes (McCulloch, 1995). Furthermore, it is always easier to claim that a productivity crisis or high unemployment are to do with lack of skills in the work force than to address the complex issues of investment, planning and management of the economy. From a 14-19 perspective, however, we cannot avoid the world of work, and as social scientists such as Bowles and Gintis have long argued, if we do not recognise it explicitly, the economy will continue to haunt us through the hidden curriculum. There is a slightly different issue here, however, that concerns links between changes in the global economy and the basis that young people have for thinking about there futures.

At some point between the ages of 14-19 most young people in industrial societies begin to think about the world of work, either through reading, or a part-time job or work experience or through parental or other role models. In some areas of this country this can mean learning that the majority of adults are out of work; in other areas, they will learn that those in jobs are far from secure and may face the consequences of a sudden lay-offs or closure or the equally sudden decision to build a Korean (or Japanese) factory in the locality. These economic instabilities (which, increasingly, can only be understood on a global scale) cannot avoid leaving their mark on how young people grow up and the meaning they give to their gender and cultural identity and to what kind of adult person and a citizen they become. It is ironic therefore that a critical understanding of economic change has such a marginal role in the curriculum.

In considering the implications of these changes for the 14-18 curriculum, I want to start from the point made in the editorial that personal and social development is about: 'developing the understandings and skills to enable (young people) to shape the world in which they live both now and in the future', and suggest that there are a number of ways in which the economic changes, I have referred to, can bear directly on this aim. Firstly there is the changing moral basis of forms of production(or business); secondly there are the cultural as well as the economic implications of globalisation, and thirdly there is the idea that in the future those who want to remain employed are going to need to be increasingly 'flexible'.

There are a number of different perspectives on the morality of production. One is the present government view (and closely in line with the view of the Adam Smith Institute, though not necessarily of Adam Smith himself!), that business is moral and a source of criteria for what is good. Hence maximising profits is always good and business principles should be applied to any situation where priorities are involved. The educational implication of this view is that business is like justice — that truth and fairness and should be part of any framework of personal development. A more traditional educational view is that business is a necessary evil and quite separate from the values like the respect for truth and toleration of differences that are associated with education. From this perspective, business is not a good in itself.

It was this latter view, sometimes taken to extremes, that the Callaghan Ruskin speech of 1976 and much recent government policy has attempted to counter. Charles Handy (1994) has a very different view of business; he argues that all the best businesses treat profits as a necessary background to doing something that they think is worthwhile and which satisfies people's needs. Interpreted simplistically, Handy's view appears somewhat naive, at least in the light of the asset stripping and down-sizing that has characterised the policies of a number of multinationals in the 1980s and 1990s. The search for evidence and arguments for and against these different versions of the morality of work in a capitalist society is one indication of the increasingly complex and ambiguous world we are preparing young people for and of the crucial role of such issues in the personal and social development of young people.

There are other indications of the educational implications of global economic changes. Two of the themes of earlier chapters: cultural diversity and tolerance and learning to trust other persons, are no longer marginal issues that schools try to equip their pupils with against the pressures of the 'real world'; they lie at the heart of leading edge business practice. For example, one of the meanings of globalisation is that the ownership of a company, the production of the goods it sells and the markets for those goods can easily be located in three different continents. In the 1950s and 1960s, American (and sometimes European) companies would dump their cheap goods on other parts of the world without caring how they were received as long as some were bought. This is less and less possible, as companies are no longer able to rely on a core of home-based sales and face more and more competition at home and abroad. (Reich, 1991). A company which wants to be successful in another part of the world needs to come to terms with different cultures in a similar way that members of a multicultural community need to learn about each other. In other words, while learning to understand other cultures and to value them needs to be part of a student's personal development, as earlier chapters in this book discuss, it can also be a potential basis for enhancing her/his employability.

Another example can be found in the new forms of advanced production such as 'stepper' factories, where the new 'machines for making microprocessors' are made and where each product is unique and there are no written procedures or fixed skills required for the production process. Production workers increasingly have to learn to trust each other, take risks and support each other when a decision goes wrong. In other words personal development can no longer be detached from employability; to be a worker in one of the new factories, one has to learn to behave morally, to be tolerant and to respect others.

The point of these examples is to argue not that capitalism has suddenly become benign, but that the developments that are shaping our economic future require similar skills, knowledge and attitudes to those that a young person wanting to shape her or his own life needs to develop. If successful twenty-first-century companies are going to be those that listen to their employees and their customers, then it is important that young people seeking to shape their lives, understand why this is so, and why it still applies relatively rarely in the UK.

9. Conclusions

I have drawn on a number of perspectives to reflect on the aim of this book, which is to reassert the importance of personal and social development in the curriculum. The implications of schools developing their own curriculum purposes were considered, and also what this might mean for specialist subject teachers. The analysis suggested a need to change our traditional concepts of a curriculum where subjects defined purposes to one based on *connective integration*, in which curriculum purposes define the role of subjects (and the limits of their role). In considering the possibilities of such a change, I suggested that in current practice we could identify a transitional model, expressed in the various attempts to make schools more effective and enhance learning. The evidence for this was that, as schools placed more emphasis on whole school policies for raising attainment, they were coming up against the limits of forms of organisation based on bureaucratic integration. Secondly, I drew on a 14-19 perspective and took account of the shaping effects of global transformation of the economy. Here my analysis would suggest that the National Curriculum needs to be extended through to 18 by developing a broad concept of a core curriculum for all students, regardless of the programme that they follow. This could be the basis of a framework to overcome the discontinuity at 16+ and the current absence of any core curriculum for students after they are 16. A number of ways have been suggested as to how such a 14-19 core might be expressed in curriculum terms; the paper by Whitty et al (1995) offers one possibility. However, no proposal for 14-19 continuity could be implemented without significant reforms to A- levels and GNVQs in their current form. Nor would any concept of personal and social development for the 14-18 age group be adequate unless complemented by a core focus on understanding economic and technological change.

Finally, if we are to start from the personal and social development of individual learners who increasingly learn to manage their own learning, we need to remember that learning, like personal development, is inescapably social. As the Finnish educationalist Engestrom puts it 'learning takes place either directly or indirectly in a *community of practice*' (1994). Engestrom recognises that *communities of practice* can refer to any social context or setting, including a school or college. A fashionable current view of an optimum community of practice is the idea of an 'educational market' in which the learner is a chooser (or a buyer). However, there are a number of problems with such a model. Firstly, although markets are social institutions, they are institutions that individualise (it is only incidental that there is interaction in a supermarket) and give priority to competitive relationships between people. They cannot therefore encourage the interactive and collaborative processes that are fundamental to learning. Secondly, despite the rhetoric of choice associated with markets, it is never possible, in practice, for learners to act like customers and 'shop around' to any great extent, even if they wanted to. As a model for linking the personal development of students to their aspirations for the future, Engestrom suggests the need to include three contexts in the aim of what he calls 'expanded learning'. The three contexts he describes are:

- criticism of the practice of the school
- discovery and use of new concepts
- practical social application

Engestrom argues that with such a model, schools can enable students and teachers to 'design and implement their own futures, as their prevailing practices show symptoms of crisis'.

With the severe cuts in budgets and various threats of industrial action, there is no doubt that in England in 1995 many teachers would agree that the education system is in a crisis. The critical tasks for teachers are both to help students with the 'sweat and toil of learning', as Gramsci put it, and to articulate for them a vision of where their learning might lead them in the future. The most debilitating effects of educational policy in the last few years have been its absence of vision and purpose. Maybe this lack of vision is a failure of imagination on the part of both politicians and educationalists, or maybe it is that educationalists have been seduced by the plausible voices of post-modernism that deny the possibility of any systematic thinking about the future. On the other hand it is possible that there are some who are more calculating and realise that without a shared vision of what they are trying to achieve, teachers in the public sector can do little more than try and make sense for their students of the endless, and often ill-thought-out initiatives coming from government.

Whichever of these accounts is nearer the truth, there are two important lessons from this book as a whole. Although the burden is on us, in every school, college and university in the country to provide a vision for our students, it cannot be done by individual institutions alone. Sally Inman and Martin Buck in their chapter on personal and social development recognise this in taking some inspiration from the proposals from HMI and the Scottish Council for the Curriculum. When we consider the 14-19 curriculum as a whole, we need the visions of every school in the country but we need also a definition of national purpose in a truly democratic National Curriculum that applies to all students, at least until they are 18 and regardless of whether they are in school or college. Whether the concept of personal and social development is, as I have suggested, a basis for such a curriculum vision or whether it is one element in developing such a vision, remains an open question that needs further analysis and debate.

Notes

(i)   A well known example of an organisational view of ethos is that adopted by the authors of *Fifteen Thousand Hours* (Rutter et al, 1979)

(ii) The idea of connectivity is explored in more detail in Young (1993) and Young et al (1994). It draws on the idea of an 'organisation as a brain' suggested in Morgan (1988)

Acknowledgements

I would like to express my thanks to Ann Hodgson, Ken Spours and Geoff Whitty for their helpful comments on earlier drafts of this chapter.

Bibliography

Bash, L. and Green, A. (Eds) (1995) *Youth, Education and Work*, World Yearbook of Education, Kogan Page

Brown, P. and Lauder, H. (1995) *Post fordist possibilities: education, training and national development* in Bash, L. and Green, A. (Eds) Youth, Education and Work, World Yearbook of Education, Kogan Page

Engestrom, (1991) *Non scolae sed vitae discimus:* Toward overcoming the encapsulation of school learning, *Learning and Instruction,* 1, 243-259

Engestrom, Y. (1994) *Training for Change: New approach to instruction and learning in working life,* ILO, Geneva

Gramsci, A. (1971) *Selections from the Prison Notebooks* (Edited and Translated by Quentin Hoare and Geoffrey Nowell Smith) Lawrence and Wishart

Mc Culloch, G. (1985) *From education to work: the case of technical schools* in Bash, L. and Green, A. (1995) op.cit.

Morgan, G. (1986) *Images of Organisation*, Sage Publications

Power, S. (1991) 'Pastoral Care as Curricular Discourse: a study in the reformulation of 'academic' schooling, *International Journal of Sociology of Education*, Vol 1 1991, p 193-208

Reich (1991) *The Work of Nations*, Simon and Schuster, London

Rowe, G. and Whitty, G. (1993) Five themes remain in the shadows *TES*, 9 April

Rutter, M. et al (1979) *Fifteen Thousand Hours*, Open Books

Spours, K. and Young, M. (1988) Beyond Vocationalism, *British Journal of Education and Work*, 1988, Vol 1

Spours, K. and Young, M. (1995) *Enhancing the Post 16 Curriculum: Value Added Perspectives,* Post 16 Education Centre Report No:10

Whitty, G., Rowe, G., and Aggleton, P., Subjects and Themes in the secondary school Curriculum *Research Papers in Education,* Vol 9, No.2 1994 p 159-181

Young, M. (1993) A Curriculum for the 21st Century, *British Journal of Educational Studies,* XXXX, Vol. 3

Young, M. et al (1994) An interim approach to unifying the post 16 curriculum in Tomlinson, S. (Ed) (1994) *Educational Reform and its Consequences,* IPPR/Rivers Oram Press

Postscript

This book is concerned with the direction of education. However, in the process of writing and especially in the later stages of editing the book, we have become increasingly aware that people outside of education are raising fundamental questions about the nature and purpose of institutions, including economic institutions, in British society. This in turn has raised further questions about the values which underpin our society as we move towards the 21st century. For example, Will Hutton, in *The State We're In,* has recently argued for a transformation of these institutions as part of the process of social and political renewal. Hutton argues for a new conception of citizenship, saying:

> Britain must complete the unfinished business of the 17th century and
> equip itself with a constitution that permits a new form of economic,
> social and political citizenship. Economic citizenship will open the
> way to reform of our financial and corporate structures; social citizen-
> ship will give us the chance of constructing an intelligent welfare state
> based on active solidarity; and political citizenship opens the way to
> political pluralism and genuine co-operation. This idea of citizenship
> could subsume differences of gender and race, and instil a sense of
> obligation to our natural environment.

Hutton stresses the need for a reformed and more *moral* society, underpinned by a system of communally agreed values embodied in social policies and institutions.

Ideas such as Hutton's remind those of us in education that the debates outlined in *Adding Value?* about the purpose and direction of the school curriculum, have to be shared more explicitly with the people who are exploring values in other, non-educational institutions and the wider society.

A period of dissatisfaction and reflection seems to be fulminating across a wide spectrum of British society. More and more groups are raising questions about the purposes and values of institutions, be they schools or financial institutions, welfare or health systems. Important issues around rights, responsibilities and democratic control are beginning to publicly debated once more. This wide, and at times contradictory, debate constantly returns to the nature and purposes of education and schooling. At the centre is the role of education in the formation of the citizens of tomorrow. The writing of this book has further convinced us of the need for a sustained national debate about the purposes and values of education and schooling as we move into the 21st century.